FROM D&M XMAS '92

WALKING & WORKING STICKS

THEO FOSSEL

Best Wishes

With a Foreword by PHIL DRABBLE

First published in Great Britain in 1986
by THE APOSTLE PRESS
119 Station Road
Beaconsfield Road
Beaconsfield
Buckinghamshire HP9 1LG

Reprinted August 1987
2nd Reprint November 1990
3rd Reprint August 1992

ISBN 1 869988 00 0 Hardback
ISBN 1 869988 01 9 Paperback

Printed and bound by
Printhaus Book Company
Northampton
for and on behalf of
Richard Netherwood Ltd.
Huddersfield

DEDICATION

This book is dedicated to my family and friends without whom life would be an empty shell.

ACKNOWLEDGEMENTS

Cover painting and drawings by John Paley
Diagrams by Paul Clark
Photographs by Julian Bembridge and the author

Thanks are due to all those friends who supported and encouraged me in this project, with particular reference to the founding members of the British Stickmakers Guild and the Stonesdale Syndicate.

Valuable comments on the manuscript were contributed by Paul Colbert and David Coulson, nor would this book look half as tidy without the very professional help from Bobby Jolowicz.

It is impossible to name all those who have helped me in my research but I must express my debt to Catherine Dike, Charlie May, Lawrie Phillips, Tom Hanson, Stuart King, Leonard Parkin, Graham Suggett, Marvin Elliott and Ken Stoodley.

None of this book would have been possible without the work of many stickmakers and stickdressers over several generations.

In the rush of getting this book completed in time for the C.L.A. Game Fair, there is bound to be someone I have left out. For this I can only apologise in advance.

CONTENTS

THE WALKING STICK

The walking stick – Not just an aid
More like a trusted friend unpaid,
A lick of varnish a polish or two
It will support you all life through,
So if in trouble No need to shout
You have a friend with a lot of clout

Marvin Morgan
St Fagan 1986

FOREWORD

In our hustling age, when automation and computers threaten to rule our lives, more and more people yearn for the old fashioned skills and simple ways of life.

For the last decade, I have been involved with a television programme. One Man and His Dog, which has introduced millions of urban folk to simple country ways and to shepherds and other craftsmen who still earn their living in delightful country by the same skills that have flourished for generations.

Occasionally we show collections of hand-carved shepherds' crooks or let viewers into the secrets of the craft of crook making by filming exponents of the art of making crooks to exhibit at country fairs or simply for the satisfaction of creative achievement.

Such exhibitions invariably attract mountains of correspondence from those who are fed-up with the pressures of modern life and long for saner and more solid values.

A good stick as a partner on a country ramble is a sure way of feeling part of the countryside. If you have made it yourself, from wood you have gathered from a hedgerow, and fashioned into a work of art, it will be a talking point with strangers and something to be proud about.

Theo Fossel is the focus of the art, the practitioners of which have formed the British Stickmakers Guild, now with a membership of 650.

To focus attention on his ancient art, he has written this informative book, in which he gives the history – and some of the folklore – of sticks and discusses the relative merits of different species of wood, ranging from alder to yew.

It is a book which will whet the appetite of every countrylover to have a sturdy stick to accompany him wherever he goes. If it is a work of art, fashioned by his own hands, it will soon be a favourite stick as well – and this book will point him in the right direction to joining the congenial band of creative stick makers.

Phil Drabble

INTRODUCTION

Cutting yourself a walking aid must be a pastime that goes back to the time when man first walked around on two legs. Indeed he probably used a stick to bring himself upright for the first time. No doubt he soon tried to change its shape by scraping it with something like a stone and progressed to embellishing it with symbols and then to carving it into shapes.

The earliest surviving 'proper' walking stick known to us was made in Hungary in about 1450 and is relief carved with historical events of the time. Walking sticks came into fashionable use in Britain only some hundred years after that and stayed in common use until earlier this century both as a useful tool and sometimes as a more or less ornate item of fashion. Its demise was almost inevitable with the development of the motorcar – where were you to put an item three feet long without getting tangled up with it in small cars like the Austin 7? The use of a car also meant less need for lengthy walking.

Longer sticks and staffs have of course been in use since earliest times and are now often associated with our mental image of travellers and pilgrims. They played a significant part in history. Saffron is reputed to have been smuggled out of Greece in a hollowed-out staff, leading to the founding of Saffron Walden and its spice industry. Similarly, silkworms were brought out of China in this way to enable silk to be produced in Europe.

A very wide range of exotic woods began to be imported for making sticks during the time of King Henry VIII, in whose reign the term 'cane' was first used. In Britain today that word implies either the use of exotic wood, such as cane, or a stick which has been reduced to a totally regular taper with no curved or angled handle.

Even though walking sticks do not wear out and are passed from one generation to the next, their manufacture continued to increase until by the late 19th century there were several manufacturers in Britain. One of these, Messrs Henry Howell and Co. of 180 City Road, London, had a staff of more than 200 workers, plus numerous outworkers and a seasoning house which alone had a frontage of 60 feet, was 100 feet in depth and four floors high. In addition to this there was the factory itself. It is hard to imagine how they brought all the material into the centre of London by horse and cart. Their catalogue, published about 1870, consisted of some 70 quarto pages of walking sticks of every type and description. Some of the materials trigger the imagination. In addition to woods such as oak, furze, cherry, 'thorn', hazel, ash and chestnut, there are such provoking names as aucuba, ceylon vine, snakewood, orange, whampoa and madagascar bamboo, and rattan. Henry Howell and Co. was taken over at the turn of the century by a company which itself has long ceased to trade. What followed is an interesting phenomenon, the parallels of which we have recently begun to experience again in this country. All the workers who were made redundant, but without the benefits of today's welfare state, had to continue to make a living somehow and most of them started up small workshops, in a shed at the back of their houses or in their local area and continued to do what they knew best: that was to make walking sticks, and as this trade began to wane they turned to making handles for the umbrella industry.

Only very recently has an interest in walking sticks and their use begun a revival, probably because of a greater amount of leisure time, a wider appreciation of the countryside, and cars which are big enough to accommodate sticks without involving major contortions. There are now an ever-increasing number of people using sticks and also making them as a hobby. Several good carvers have turned their hand to embellishing sticks, and some quite excellent work is being produced.

Stickmaking also encompasses the much more specialised field of stickdressing. This term relates strictly and only to the bending (through heat) and subsequent carving of thermoplastic horns such as ram, buffalo, (and to a lesser extent ox, goat and others) into stick handles, principally shepherds' crooks. Stickdressing does not include work in staghorn since this material is more like bone and cannot be bent by heat, or any other means. At its best, stickdressing is more an artform in its own right than a mere craft, particularly when performed by such masters as George Snaith, Edward Henderson, Norman

Tulip, Rob Little, Leonard Parkin and others. There are also a great many up-and-coming stickdressers so there is no fear that this art will die out in the foreseeable future.

The fact that both stickmaking and stickdressing are experiencing a thorough revival is evidenced by the formation early in 1984 of The British Stickmakers Guild. Its prime function is, for the first time, to provide a focal point for the exchange of information on this very wide subject and to provide a link for a great many stickmakers, all of whom had previously been working in almost total isolation. The existence of a need for such an organisation was proved by the fact that nearly 500 members had joined within the first 12 months, thus enabling two editions of the *Stickmaker* magazine to be published, and the first-ever National Stick Competition was arranged for the spring of 1985. This has become an annual event.

There are no limits to stickmaking other than those set by a maker's imagination and by the practical aspects of using a stick. No matter how well carved and beautiful a stick may be, there remains the fact that it must be useable. That is to say, it must provide a third point of balance and come well to hand. Even the most artistically carved stick is useless if the carving has projections which 'fire the hand' or which will break off the first time the stick is dropped, as any stick is bound to be sooner or later. This problem also applies to the thousands of resin-cast handles which are available these days: they are too brittle and will not stand up to the job. There are, however, other handles in modern synthetic materials which do serve the purpose very well.

This book has been written because, despite the vast number of books published on just about every subject under the sun, there is not one book available which gives the potential stickmaker information on the full range of the craft. Stickdressing has been covered but not to the extent of listing the very wide range of native woods we have available in this country.

Remember, as a final thought, that you do not have to be old or infirm to carry a stick. It makes a jolly good companion, can keep all sorts of dogs at bay . . . and doesn't even talk back !

WOODS

The most commonly used woods for walking sticks are hazel, ash, chestnut and blackthorn, but there are a great many more. The following is a far from complete list of woods which can be used for making sticks, together with some which should be avoided. The list is restricted to trees which grow wild in Britain since these are the ones most likely to be available to British stickmakers. The list is almost endless. A London firm specialising in sticks and umbrellas was once commissioned to make a walking stick from every kind of wood growing naturally in Britain. They are understood to have eventually given up at over seventy sticks.

The descriptions given must always be general ones since great variations can be found, for example in bark colours, because of either location, climate, soil, sub-species or heavy algae growth which prevents the normal bark colour from developing.

ALDER – *Alnus glutinosa*
This native British tree is most common along the banks of streams and on damp ground but seldom grows on dry ground. It is widespread throughout the British Isles.

It is easily recognised by its almost black bark with horizontal blotches on older wood. The leaves in summer are broad and almost round. The twigs in winter are dark brown, with slightly fuzzy buds, brownish-grey catkins and fir-cone-like fruit pods from the previous summer.

The wood is easily carved and slightly yellow in colour. It is very water resistant when seasoned, very lightweight and does not easily split.

Alder is not good for making sticks, being very light in weight, although for some that may be a desirable feature.

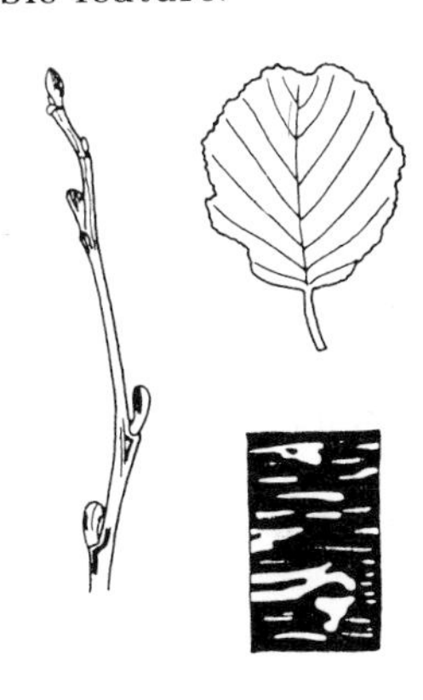

Alder

APPLE – *Malus sp*
Like most other fruit woods, this makes excellent sticks, so never burn your tree prunings before sorting through them. The wood itself is rather hard but can be carved well into crook handles. On exposure to daylight it often develops an attractive pink tinge.

ASH, COMMON ASH – *Fraxinus excelsior* (for Mountain Ash *see* Rowan)
One of the most easily recognised trees by its grey bark and, in winter, by its prominent velvet black buds.

The wood is well suited to making sticks because of its strength and resistance to splitting. Surprisingly, ash is a relative of the olive tree. It grows well all over the British Isles and has always been a good source for tool handles in that it is strong, elastic and easily bent to shape after steaming.

Ash is still grown from seed specifically for use as sticks. So-called cross-head walking sticks are grown by digging up the two-year-old seedling, trimming it back to a bud and re-planting it horizontally. The bud then grows into an upright shank with the rootstock forming a very strong, naturally shaped handle rather like an upside-down 'L'. Unlike steamed handles, these will never straighten out if left in the damp since they are already in a relaxed state.

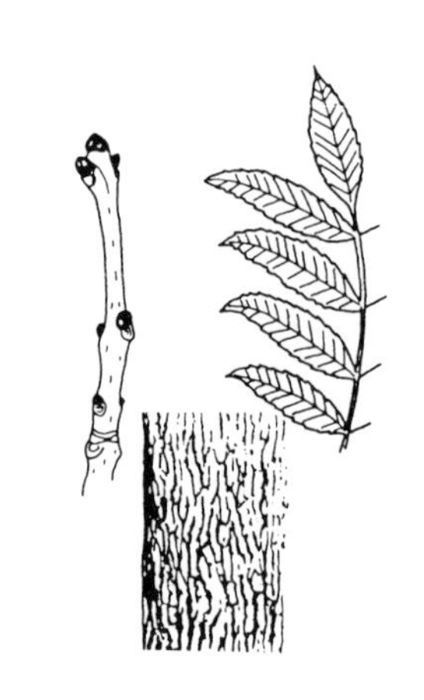

Ash

BEECH – *Fagus sylvatica*
Although this species is native to the British Isles, it does not naturally reproduce itself in northern counties because the seed will not ripen. It is, however, planted throughout Britain as a seedling.

Its smooth grey bark is very typical on older growth. Young twigs are slender with slightly zig-zag growth. Very slender pointed buds sit on stalks which are heavily ringed.

The wood is heavy and even textured. Although it has many commercial uses, particularly for furniture making, it makes very indifferent walking sticks.

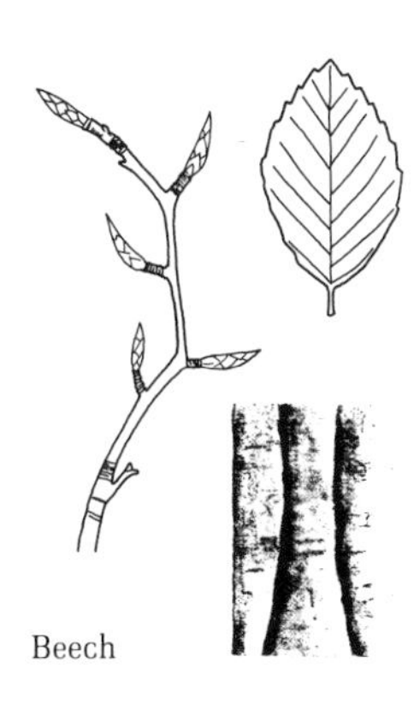

Beech

BIRCH – *Betula pendula* (Silver Birch)
This tree can sometimes confuse people because young growth has a brown-coloured bark. The typical white bark does not develop until the tree is some years old.

Birch has always been regarded as a 'protective tree', and its presence in the house was thought to ward off the 'evil eye'. At one time 'broomstick' or 'besom' weddings were considered as binding as a church wedding. The couple had to jump one after the other over a birch broom held up against the doorway of the house and were then considered wedded.

Birch is one of the hardiest trees in the world and is generally one of the earliest colonisers of any ungrazed land. The wood is pale brown, soft and even grained: heart and sapwood are the same colour. It rots easily out of doors but makes very good walking sticks, which are light and yet very strong. Both the bark and the peeled/fumed stick are very effective.

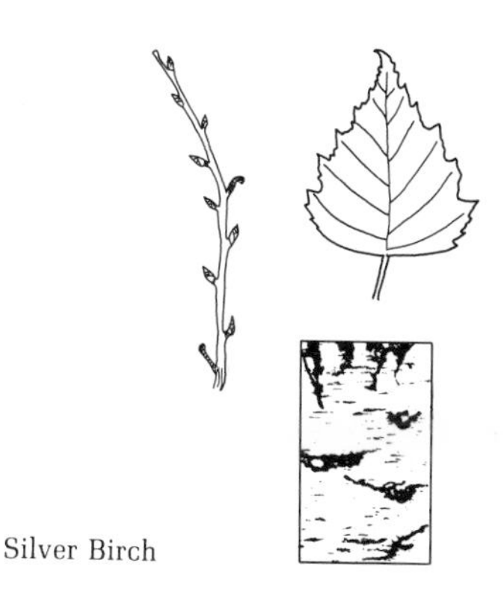

Silver Birch

BLACKTHORN – *Prunus spinosa* (bullister or slae in Scotland)
Is a native bush of Britain and perhaps best known as the origin of sloe gin, that excellent reviver after spending a wet and slimy day in winter cutting sticks. It is nowadays used as the raw material for

making the club-shaped Irish shillelagh although originally this used to be an oak throwing stick, as many a hare and other game found out to their cost.

In some parts of the British Isles the blackthorn has a particular mystique about it and is generally considered the ultimate wood for walking sticks. Whether this reputation is fully deserved is debatable since blackthorn does tend to be on the heavy side. Even so, there is nothing to compare with the feel of a well-balanced blackthorn stick or to surpass the richness of the red, deep red, bark once it has been varnished, but hopefully not stained. The Irish prefer their blackthorn sticks to be black and I have heard it said that this is because they used to bury them in peat bogs and/or hang them over their open fires to cure them.

Seasoning of blackthorn is quite critical since it does tend to develop longitudinal shakes if cut at the wrong time or brought indoors too soon.

The ultimate blackthorn, perhaps one in a thousand or more, has totally regular knobs, each with three spines. The knobs should be closely spaced and have an indentation above each, known as St Patrick's Thumbprint. Even taper and thus good balance are also vital factors. Such sticks may be valued at up to £200 each.

It is sometimes difficult to know if one is faced with true blackthorn, damson or wild plum, which are all very closely related. One fairly reliable test when the wood is still green, is to scrape back a little of the bark at the roots and after a while the inner cambrium should turn bright orange.

Blackthorn tends to spread mostly through root suckers. It is always well worth while, if the situation and the soil allow, to dig down to the root. More often than not this will be found to form a perfect natural cross handle. Be careful not to tear into the wood when cutting it loose.

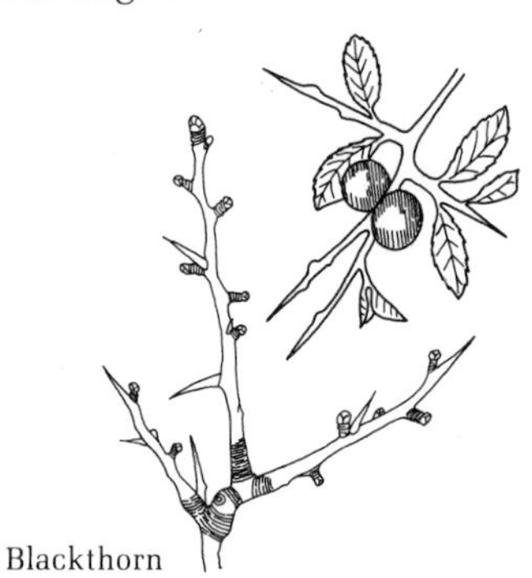

Blackthorn

BOG OAK – *Quercus sp*
This may seem out of place in a list such as this, but some spectacular crook handles can be made from it. Most bog oak is somewhere between 20 000 and 80 000 years old and therefore needs special consideration when working it.

It should be worked whilst still wet and kept in a plastic bag when it is not actually being worked on. It carves extremely easily when wet but becomes as hard as iron once it has dried out. Drying must be done very slowly and carefully to prevent shakes from developing. It may take a year or more fully to dry out bog oak, during which time it helps to apply liberal coats of boiled linseed oil regularly, but no varnish.

Bog oak will shrink considerably – by about 25% to 30% across the grain in drying. Allow for this when cutting out or you may find that your joint diameter of, say, an inch has shrunk to less than $\frac{3}{4}$ in.

The colour of bog oak can vary from near jet black from the Cambridgeshire Fens to a brown from Cumbria.

BOX – *Buxus sempervirens*
This small native tree is rarely found growing wild except on some chalk hills in Surrey. It is now most frequently found as an evergreen hedge or shaped bush in gardens. Traditionally box was used as a decoration between February and Easter.

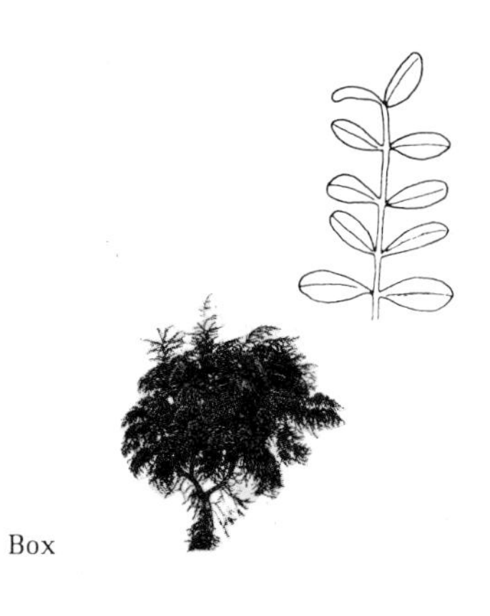

Box

The wood is yellow, very hard, fine grained and dense. It is used a great deal in making small wooden items and also in wood blocks for printing. Along with hawthorn it is the traditional wood for turning the pipes for Scottish bagpipes.
The bark is light brown and stringy but turns darker with age. Box is an evergreen with very small shiny leaves, dark on top,

lighter underneath and with a distinct notch at the end of the leaf.

The wood is well suited to making sticks but it is difficult to find suitably shaped lengths. Box is almost too rare and valuable to use for making a stick other than for carving handles.

BRAMBLE – *Rubus fruticosus* (Blackberry)
There are many hundreds of species in Britain. Some are upright, some creeping and others arching. I have never yet come across any which had the right stiffness for stickmaking.

Bramble

BRIAR – *Erica arborea*
Strictly speaking the term briar should apply only to the tree heather but is commonly used in describing the dog rose (*see* Wild Rose). The tree heather is found mainly in the Mediterranean area where its root stock is used for making pipes and other fancy items. The wood is heavily figured, dark brown after exposure to light and close-grained.

True briar is too valuable to use for complete sticks but several wood carvers in this country produce the most delightful stickheads from briar.

BROOM – *Sarothammus scoparius*
Although this plant does not generally grow more than six feet high, it does provide excellent sticks and grows all over the British Isles except in the Orkney and Shetland Isles. It has always been regarded as a symbol of good luck and plenty because of its profusion of yellow flowers in May and June. Its earlier botanical name was *Planta genista*. Broom was the symbol of the Duke of Anjou, the father of Henry II of England, who adopted it as his family name – hence the Plantagenets. It has

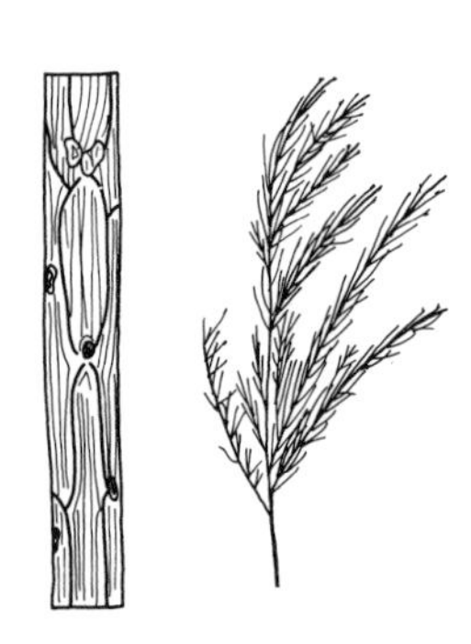
Broom

branches and twigs which, though they stay green, lose their leaves in winter. Twigs are pure green but branches and stems are tinged with deep magenta and have very characteristic, oblong, thin raised markings between buds. Very good lightweight sticks can be made from broom with or without its bark.

CABBAGE STICK

CABBAGE — *Brassica oleracea longata* (Long Jacks, Free Cabbage, Giant Cabbage, Jersey Cabbage) It may seem strange to list a cabbage among woods suitable for sticks but this variety of cabbage or kale does produce woody stems strong enough to make walking sticks. They have recently been revived as a well-known souvenir for visitors to the Channel Island of Jersey.

Seeds are available in Great Britain for this extraordinary plant which is winter hardy and will grow to a height of over 12 feet in two years. As a friend of mine put it 'just think of those poor caterpillars'! The seeds are planted in August — the best time being the first full moon in that month! The plant is used to provide fodder for animals, the

Cabbage

leaves being picked progressively up the stems as they mature.

The walking sticks are seasoned for only a few months and finished either with a metal or turned wood knob.

CASTANEA — another name (the Latin one in fact) for Sweet Chestnut.

CHERRY — *Prunus avium* (Gean)
The wild cherry or gean grows all over Britain but is more common in the South. The smaller Bird Cherry is more frequently found in Scotland and Wales. Both are planted often as nurse trees in forestry and removed once the maincrop trees have fully established themselves.

Cherry bark is a dull purplish-grey with horizontal bands of pale brown and with corky breathing pores. It makes excellent walking sticks, and the bark can almost rival that of blackthorn in beauty. It is unusual to remove the bark on cherry wood sticks, and there is much to be lost by so doing. Occasionally one can find cherry on which the bark has turned almost silver with grey horizontal bands in it. This may be a sign of the first onset of disease or fungal attack, but in those I have found the wood appeared perfectly sound.

Like all fruit trees, cherry wood is strong with darker heartwood and has a most attractive lustre. It sometimes seems to have streaks of green and makes good handle-carving wood

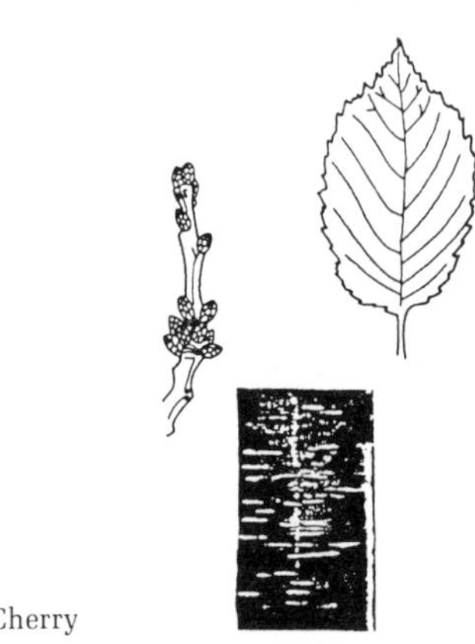

Cherry

CHESTNUT — *Castanea sativa* (Sweet Chestnut, Castanea sticks)
This was reputed to have been imported into Britain by the Romans. It now grows wild here but is rare further north and does not set good fruit except in southern counties.

This wood should not be confused with horse chestnut which is generally used for panelling and cleft fencing stakes. Sweet chestnut is very suitable for walking sticks – in fact that universal beast the National Health Stick is made from it. There is even a British Standards (No. BS 5181:1975) covering it.

The shoots of sweet chestnuts have stout round buds which develop into large, broad, oval leaves with saw-tooth edges. The smooth brown bark of young growth becomes grey with age, deeply ridged on the trunk and often spiralling.

It is one of the traditional coppice trees. The smaller shoots are harvested every two to three years for stickmaking. Chestnut sticks are usually made without bark and fumed or scorched. If the bark is left on the stick it becomes almost black on finishing with varnish.

So-called Congo or Pearl-Congo sticks are sweet chestnut which have been artificially wounded during growth. The resulting scar tissue in the wood underneath adds considerably to the appearance of any stick made from it.

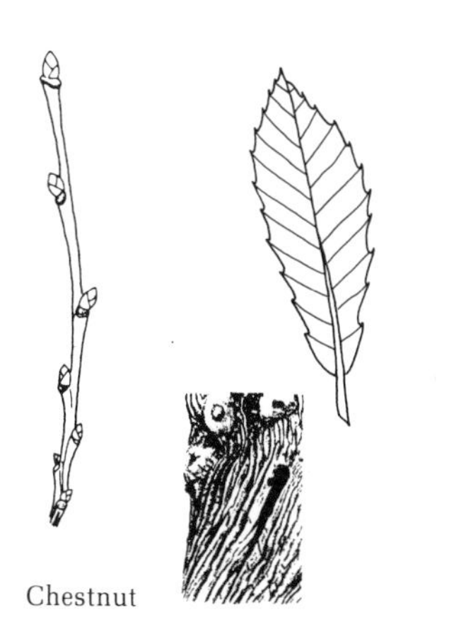

Chestnut

CONIFERS

The timber from these is known technically as 'softwood'. The terms explain why generally speaking they are not much used in the making of sticks. Most conifers have great value to the forester but few are native species. For the most part they do not coppice, and their growth has too many knots and is too heavily tapered. An exception to this is our British yew.

CORNEL CHERRY – *Cornus mas*

This is the hardest wood found in Europe and was much used in days gone by for making arrows, spears and javelins. It is closely related to dogwood.

Great medicinal properties were attributed to the fruit, which was reputed to prevent dysentery and other bowel disorders. The tree was introduced into Britain in about the 16th century from south-east Europe.

It can grow to a tree about 25 feet high, but it more usually forms just a shrub with slightly drooping branches. The leaves are quite distinct with three to five forward running veins each side of the central rib. Twigs form branches opposite each other. The bark is dark brown becoming scaly on older growth. Yellow blossoms flower in early spring, but there are several cultivated varieties.

When obtainable, cornel cherry makes one of the best sticks, usually with the bark removed.

CRAB APPLE — *Malus pumila/sylvestris*
This spiny tree is the parent of all our domestic apple trees and provides the rootstock onto which many cultivated varieties are grafted. The crab apple has grown wild in Britain since the Ice Age and can really be regarded as a native tree. It rarely grows over 30 feet in height and is most frequently found in hedgerows and neglected corners.

The wood, like cherry and other fruit wood, is ideal for carving (though somewhat hard), and for turning. It is often used for mallets and golf club heads. Walking sticks made from it are very attractive in that they often show a regular zig-zag growth between nodes. The bark on young material suitable for sticks is dark.

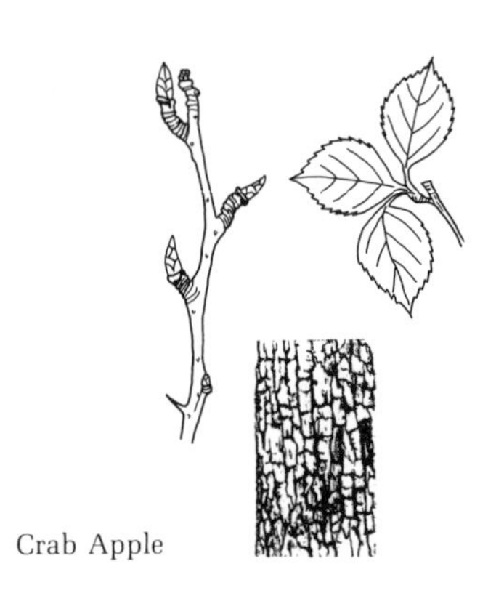
Crab Apple

DOG ROSE — *see* Wild Rose

DOGWOOD — *Cornus sanguinea* (Wax Tree, Dog Tree, Dog Berry)
A shrub which may occasionally grow into a small tree about ten feet high. The most easily recognised parts of this plant are the small blood-red twigs and in autumn the leaves, which also turn crimson red. It occurs mainly on chalk and limestone soils, often very quickly invading abandoned pasture and downlands through seeds in bird droppings and then

by suckering from the parent plant. It also coppices well.

Dogwood has always been closely associated with country life. One rhyme stated : 'When dogwood flowers appear, frost will not again be here'. Meat skewers (dogs) were made from it, as were mill-cogs, pestles, lace bobbins and wheelspokes. The berries were used for making lamp oil. It makes first-rate sticks, though they are on the heavy side. The varnished bark has very distinctive thin red vertical veins within an overall grey colour.

Dogwood

ELDER – *Sambucus nigra*
This large native bush is found all over the British Isles and is almost regarded as a weed. It may seem an unlikely choice for stickmaking but the wood is very hard and is often used as a substitute for boxwood, ivory and, when dyed black, for ebony.

Elder has long been associated with witches. It was considered unlucky to bring it into the house, but a bush planted nearby would protect the inhabitants against witches.

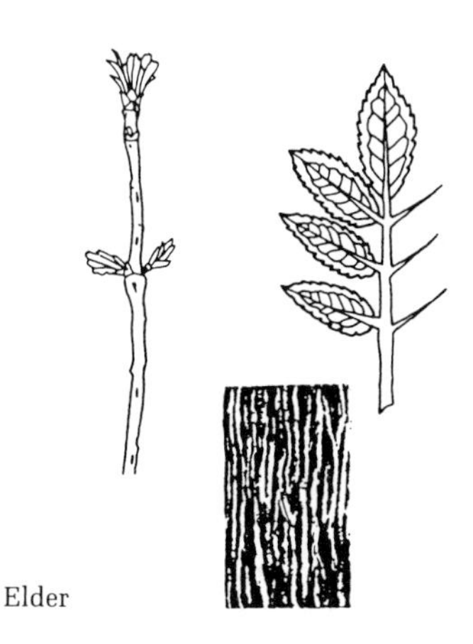

Elder

Walking sticks made from elder can be very attractive when peeled carefully. Only very young growth of about one or two years is too pithy to use. The regularly spaced nodes and irregular grooving in the peeled wood are quite distinctive. Once seasoned the wood is markedly yellow and very strong. At one time it was extensively used for the handles of fishing rods.

ELM, ENGLISH – *Ulmus procera*
The origins of this tree, generally thought typical of the British countryside, are not clear. Some claim it was introduced by the Romans, whilst others believe it to have developed from the native wych elm.

What is left of this blighted tree does make good sticks. It throws up suckers which have an attractively ridged bark, almost cork-like. The wood itself is still available but getting scarcer and is probably the most reliable for carved handles and crooks. It is the least likely of all woods in this country to split, which is why it is the traditional material for Windsor chair seats.

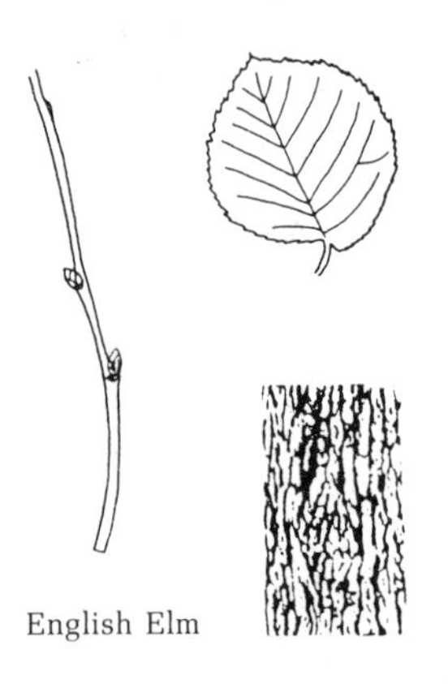
English Elm

ELM, WYCH – *Ulmus glabra* (Scots Elm)
This native tree is found usually further north and in Scotland. Unlike other elms it reproduces itself by seed and not by suckers. This means it is more resistant to Dutch elm disease, which incidentally came from North America but was first identified by the Dutch, who were then blamed for it because it was named after them.

Being very difficult to split, elm is the perfect wood for furniture and wagon wheels. 'Wych' refers to the Anglo-Saxon word for 'pliable' describing its twigs. It has a much lighter sapwood and is lighter grained than English elm but is otherwise comparable to it.

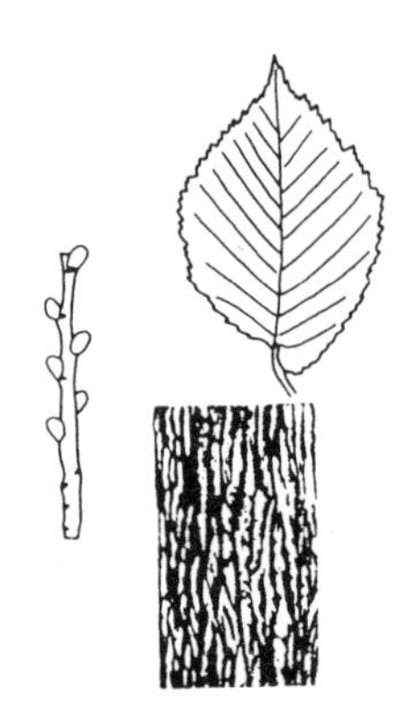
Scots Elm

GORSE – *Ulex europaeus* (Furze, Whin)
This very prickly plant is widespread throughout Britain on acid, sandy soil even in exposed windy locations. It was often used

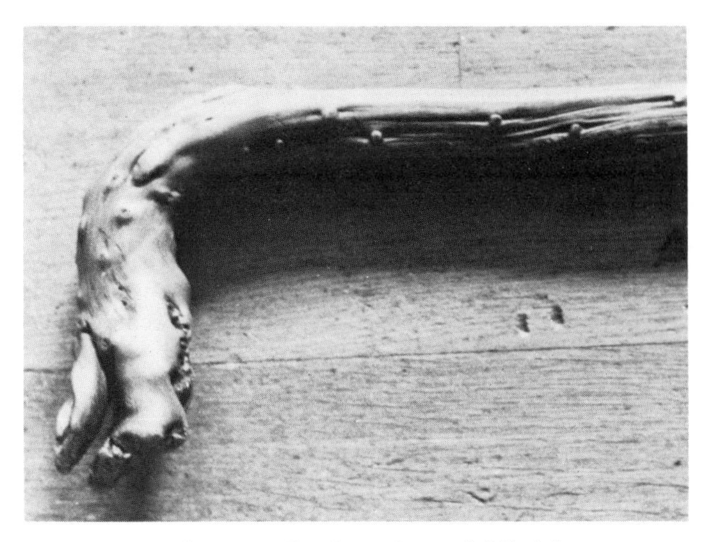

Gorse or Furze makes an excellent heavy-duty stick full of character.

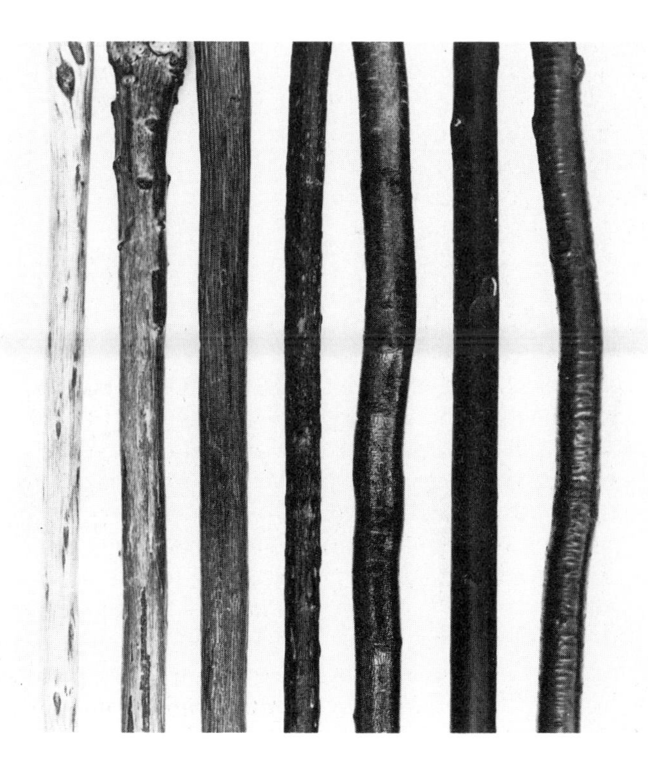

Peeled Gorse, Peeled Birch, Peeled Oak, Bark Dogrose, Bark Rowan, Bark Sweet Chestnut and Bark Cherry as an impenetrable cattle fence or planted near houses for hanging out washing. It is often now found on roadside verges. The only practical uses for gorse wood are as fuel for village bakers (because it gives a very high heat), and in making walking sticks, for which it is one of the best woods.

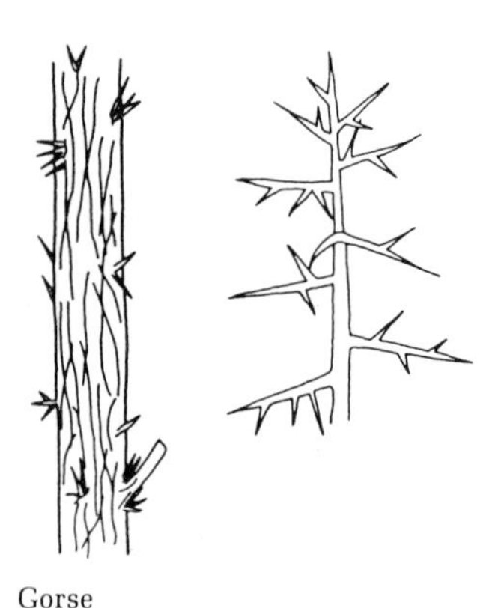

Gorse

The wood itself is very hard, dense and fibrous. As it grows it forms characteristic twists in the wood, mostly around the root area. A personal theory is that this is related to the ability of the bush to right itself very quickly after being flattened by snow.

It is rather difficult to steam and bend gorse, but not impossible if care is taken. What sets it apart as a walking stick is not only the twists but also the grain of the wood exposed after peeling. The bark itself is not worth retaining.

Gorse used to be cut by gypsies and traditionally sold on Derby Day on Epsom Common as 'gypsie furze sticks'. I do not know of anybody still making these sticks.

HAWTHORN, COMMON – *Crataegus monogyna* (Whitethorn, May, Quickthorn)

Common Hawthorn

HAWTHORN, MIDLAND – *Crataegus oxycanthoides* (Whitethorn, May, Quickthorn)

These very common small trees are found all over Britain in hedgerows and spinneys. They have strong magical associations and are generally used for celebrating the return of summer. Among the superstitions relating to hawthorn is the following rhyme:

Beware of the oak
It draws the stroke.
Avoid the ash
It courts the flash.
Creep under the thorn
It will save you from harm.

The wood itself is red-brown in the heartwood with a pale sapwood which is often marked with brown irregular stripes which look almost like flattened worm runs. It has long been one of the traditional woods used for Scottish bagpipes.

It makes first-rate sticks but the bark is rather too dull to be interesting and does not take stain well. Shaving or peeling and then fuming is very effective. The underbark is also very attractive after the outer bark has been carefully sanded away.

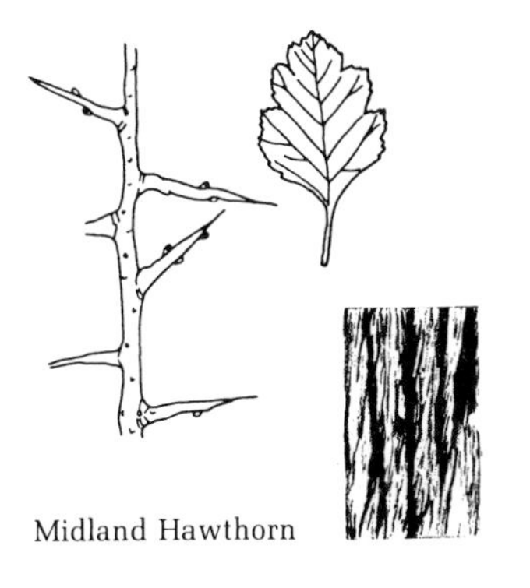

Midland Hawthorn

HAZEL – *Corylus avellana*

One of the most common bushes throughout almost the whole of the British Isles which has been used since prehistoric times for a great variety of applications such as thatching, wattle and daub, and coracles and even for reinforcing paths across peat bogs.

It grows to a height of some 12 to 15 feet and has been grown for centuries as a coppice crop. Once seen, the bark of hazel is easily recognised again, as is the shape of the bush and its habit of throwing up new shoots from the stem base. The characteristic catkins appear quite early in spring. These are actually the male flowers, the female flowers being very small buds close to the twig, marked with red tassels.

This is another very magical plant which is associated with fire and fertility. Small twigs are said to protect houses from lightning. Hazel forks are, of course, the traditional tool of the water diviner.

Hazel is arguably the most common wood used for making walking sticks. Not only is the wood relatively light in weight and strong once seasoned but also hazel rods grow in a way that requires very little further straightening. With a little care in seasoning, hazel can be cut at virtually any time of the year, though the period of maximum sap flow in spring and early summer should be avoided if possible.

The bark colour of hazel can vary greatly in the younger growth, of interest to stickmakers. It can range from a deep dark brown to what looks almost like a silver coating. I have not yet discovered a reason for these variations. Old hands at stickdressing 'up north' maintain that the silver hazel is much stronger.

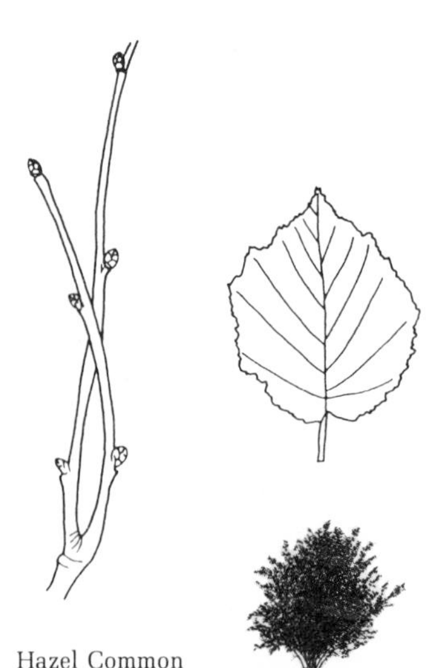

Hazel Common

HAZEL, CORKSCREW – *Corylus avellana contorta* (Contorted Hazel)
This is a variety of hazel often grown in gardens. It is nearly always grafted on to common hazel rootstock, and grows with very twisted and contorted branches. If you can bear to cut out some shoots, they make very eye-catching sticks such as the one used by Sir Harry Lauder. Naturally, no attempt should be made to straighten the shanks entirely but it may be necessary to bend them slightly to get good balance in the stick.

HOLLY – *Ilex aquifolium*
This easily recognised tree is very hardy and will grow in the toughest conditions, but not on wet soils. The shiny dark leaves with their spines on the edge together with the typical red berries have always been a symbol of eternal life and had strong associations with Christmas. They were used to guard against evil and destruction.

The wood is ivory white though it will sometimes show light grey patches. It is close grained and needs careful seasoning since, like elm, it has the tendency to 'move' after a long time. The bark, which is attractively green when young, becomes grey in more mature wood and is notoriously difficult to season without wrinkles developing. This then means that once in use the wrinkles will flake and look most unsightly. For this reason one rarely finds holly sticks which have not been peeled or shaved.

There is a method of preserving the bark which requires the stick to be washed down after cutting, dried and then varnished the very week it was cut. This means that the moisture in the stick can evaporate only very slowly and that there is about a 50/50 chance of the bark's setting smooth and tight. It follows that the stick must be seasoned for much longer than normal; this method has a better chance with wood cut in mid-winter.

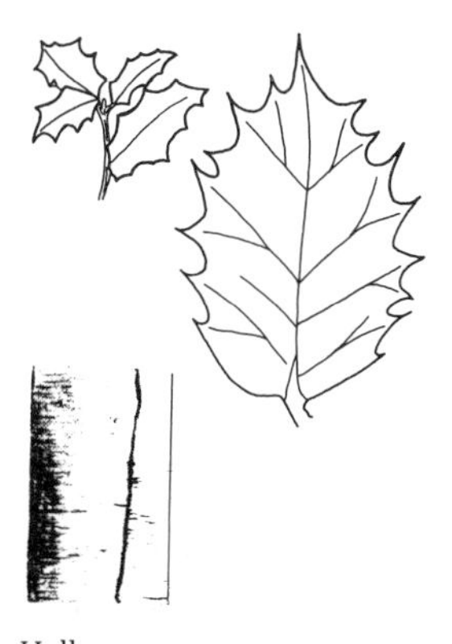

Holly

Shaved or reduced holly sticks can be stained or fumed to give an effect that looks like a watermark in the wood. For this purpose it is advisable to cut shanks which are considerably thicker than the intended stick. Plenty of knobs and bumps are good here because the interesting pattern appears where growth rings are shaved across.

HONEYSUCKLE – *Lonicera pericynemum* (Woodbine)

This climbing plant is not normally used for making sticks, but deserves a mention because it does produce perhaps the most sought-after type of stick. It climbs, always in a clockwise spiral, up any wooden stem within reach to a height of 20 feet or more. Once established on a host the wiry shoot constricts the soft tissues of its supporting plant causing severe distortions. Whilst the forester clears away honeysuckle, any stickmaker will treasure it for making very distinctive walking sticks.

Honeysuckle is the only plant which will cause this

'barley sugar' effect and will distort almost any type of tree, although I have never found it on holly.

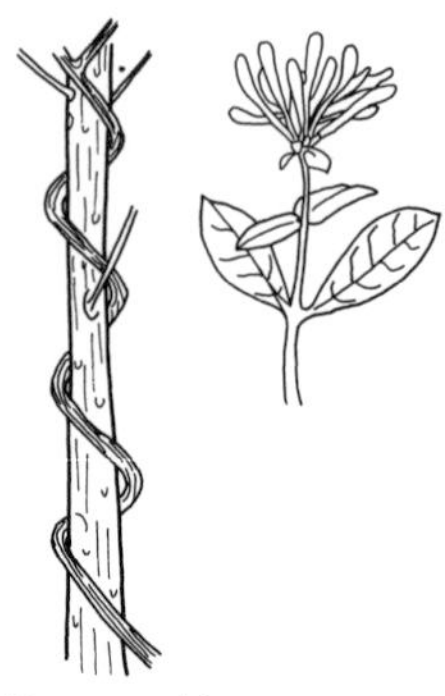

Honeysuckle

HORNBEAM – *Carpinus betulus*

The name indicates this tree's strong wood which has traditionally been used for chopping blocks, mallets, skittles and wheel spokes. It is only found growing wild in southern England but was once widely planted in certain areas for coppice and pollarding, although as a tree it will grow to a height of some 80 feet.

The mature trunk has a smooth silver-grey bark which is deeply fluted into the wood. On young shoots the pale brown buds lie tightly against the twig.

This tough wood is ideally suited for stickmaking when it is available.

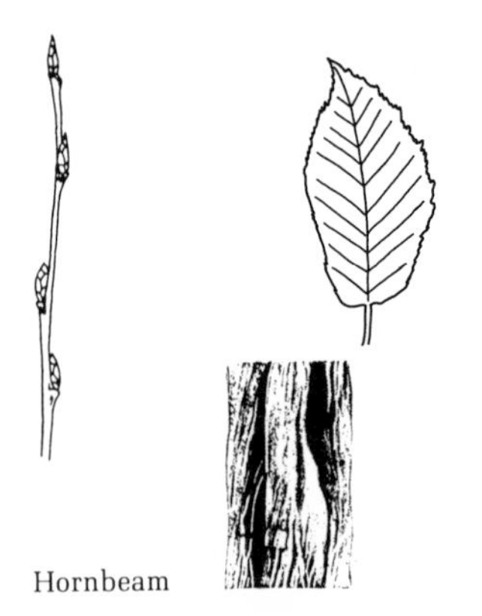

Hornbeam

IVY – *Hedera helix*

Although ivy is of course a climbing plant, walking sticks have been made from it. After careful seasoning and preparation it makes very light but strong sticks. The bark tends to flake and needs to be peeled.

Folklore has it that ivy is a kindly plant and that it stands for femininity because of its 'clinging habit'. It is also reputed to keep demons from houses at Christmas.

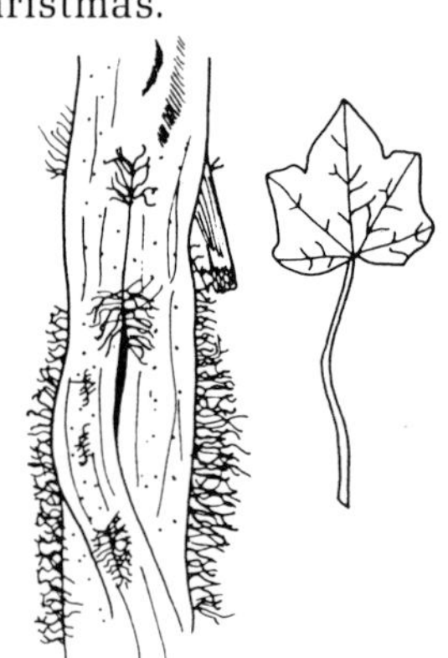

Ivy

LABURNUM – *Laburnum anagyroides*
This tree, which rarely grows to more than 30 feet in height, was introduced into Britain in the 16th century and is now one of the most popular and easily grown in gardens.

The wood of a suitable size for stickmaking is cream-coloured but turns almost pea green on being cut and has what is best described as a 'distinctive' smell (not to say nasty). Twigs and the smooth mature bark are brown with many small breathing pores. The bases of buds and twigs are notable for having a multi-ringed collar of wrinkled bark.

The wood is used for decorative carving, for turnery and for making musical instruments. It is a hard wood with a fine lustrous grain. Very rarely seen is laburnum burr, which is much lighter in colour but spectacular in its very tightly curled grain.

I have not seen laburnum used very often for stick shanks but Tom Hanson has carved some absolutely splendid stick handles from laburnum burr.

LIME – *Tilia sp*
This is the tallest broad-leaved tree in Britain, thought to have been introduced by the Romans. It grows vigorously and can live for up to 500 years. The wood from lime is much sought after for carving, model making and other applications where a light and soft wood with an absolutely even grain is required.

Tradition has it that patients suffering from epilepsy who sat under a lime tree were much improved. Bearing in mind

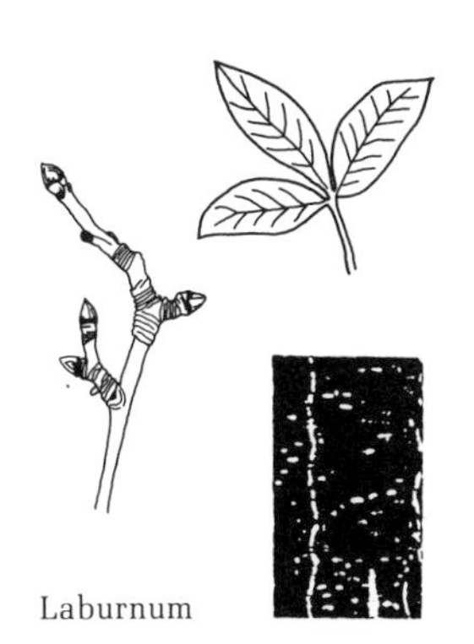

Laburnum

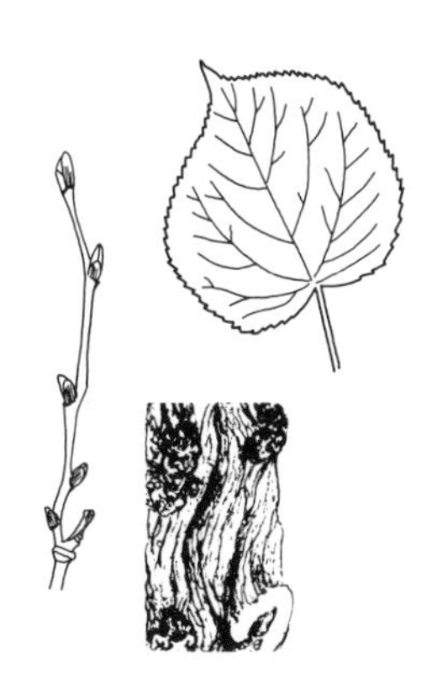

Lime

the problems with sticky aphid droppings under lime trees, I would have thought that patients would be immobilised for good!

Young shoots of lime are generally far too light and weak to make sticks, but very good handles can be carved from mature timber.

MAPLE, FIELD — *Acer campestre*
A tree most commonly found in hedgerows of southern England, large mature trees being rare. It is much sought after for its decorative 'birds eye' burr for use in furniture veneer. This distinctive figuring is found in knots formed on the trunk. Normal wood is faintly brown, hard and compact.

The mature bark on branches and the trunk forms characteristic narrow cork-like ridges

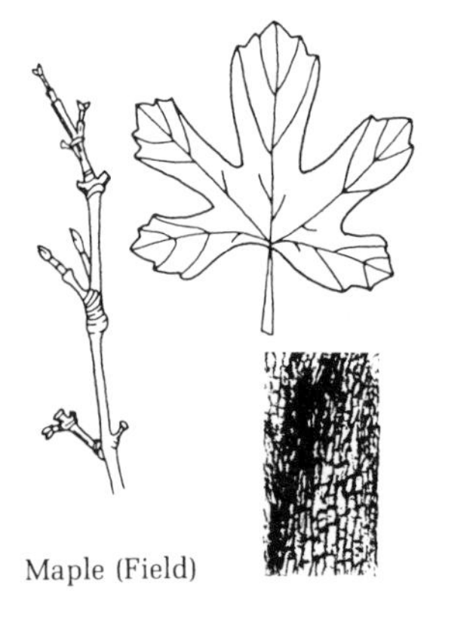
Maple (Field)

along them. It is unlikely that this very light wood from young growth will make good sticks, nor is the bark firm enough.

OAK, COMMON — *Quercus robur*

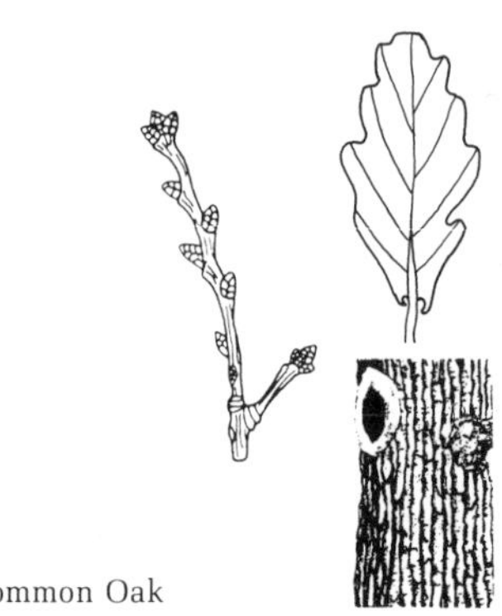
Common Oak

OAK, SESSILE — *Quercus petraea*
These two British trees can cross-pollinate, producing hybrid forms. Several other species of oak have been introduced from abroad. Of these the Holm Oak is notable for being an evergreen. The oak has long been considered the king of British trees and was even held sacred by the Druids. There are still customs in many towns and villages all over Britain which centre on the oak.

The wood of oak has characteristic radial lines across the annual rings. It is hard, dense and has long been used where these qualities are important such as for shipbuilding and in houses. The buds on twigs are set alternately and in a cluster at the tip. Young bark is smooth but soon develops lengthwise cracks, which on old wood become deep fissures.

Oak coppices well and makes first-rate distinctive sticks. Keeping the bark on is difficult if not impossible and rather pointless since it is very unattractive. On the other hand, once the bark is removed, the surface of the exposed wood has typical ridging. Being a very dense wood, oak sticks tend to be on the heavy side.

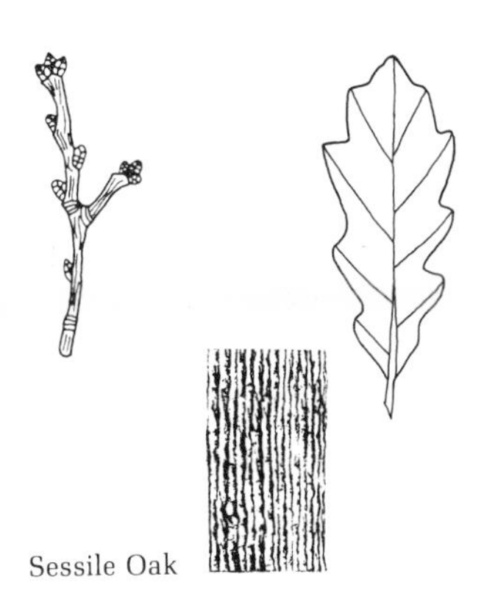

Sessile Oak

PLUM, WILD — *Prunus domestica*
This occasionally appears in hedgerows and copses where children or animals have dropped the stone of an orchard plum. The seeds of these rarely breed true and have generally half reverted to wild plum. As opposed to its nearest relative, the blackthorn, wild plum does not have spines.

The bark on young growth is green changing to a rich brown with age. Like blackthorn it spreads by throwing suckers from roots, which is of course ideal for the stickmaker. The wood is pale brown and with maturity develops a core of reddish heartwood. It is hard and dense.

POPLAR – *Populus sp*
A tree native to Britain. Although most species of poplar throw suckers very freely and are also very easily rooted simply by pushing a length of branch into damp ground, their soft mushy wood is not thought to be a good choice for making sticks.

PRIVET – *Ligustrum vulgare*
Wild privet is found in southern England in hedges and on waste ground. It is best known though as a garden hedge. This shrub which, like ash, is a member of the olive family, rarely grows taller than about ten feet. The

leaves are not truly evergreen and look rather dull. In the wild plant they are larger than in the cultivated variety, spaced further apart and have a red tint.

The wood is white and hard, well suited to stickmaking. Cutting time is critical since the bark easily wrinkles during seasoning and will then form unsightly flakes when the stick is used.

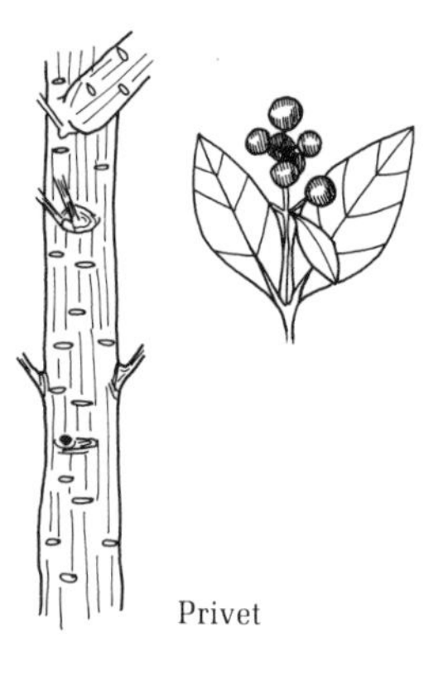

Privet

RHODODENDRON – *Rhododendron ponticum*
This most common and hardy variety of rhododendron is an escapee from gardens, which has spread freely from seed and is now most difficult to eradicate. It is an evergreen with oval shiny leaves about three to four inches long. The bark is fibrous with loose grey flakes. Under the flakes it is light brown with a slightly orange tinge.

The wood is pale brown with a slightly orange-to-yellow tinge. If you can find branches of sufficient length they will make very good light but strong sticks. It helps to sandpaper down to the underbark.

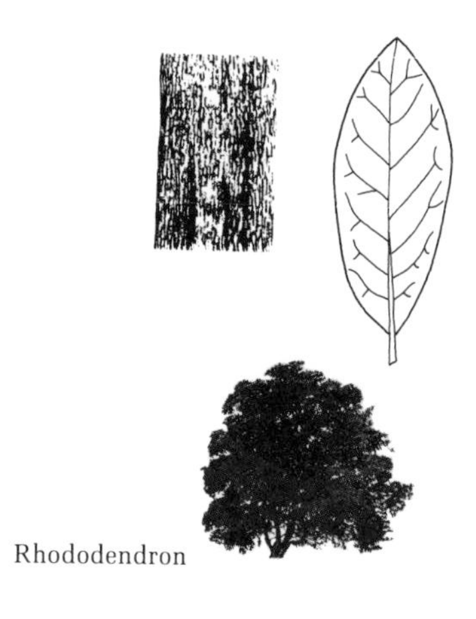

Rhododendron

ROWAN – *Sorbus aucuparia* (Mountain Ash, Quickbeam, Witchen, Quicken Tree)
The rowan is more commonly found in the north and central hilly areas of Britain and is a very hardy tree. It has long been connected with superstitions about witchcraft and was planted often outside houses and in churchyards to keep witches at bay.

Rowan has strong and

very flexible wood which was once widely used for tool handles and for carving small items. It even served as a substitute for yew in longbows and was used as the springbow in chairbodgers' lathes.

The bark is grey-brown and smooth, even on old growth, with noticeable pores. The buds in winter are very large, oval and purple in colour with a long point. It is one of the traditional woods used for carving one-piece crooks in Wales, not only because the wood is ideal but also because of its association with protection against evil. It follows then that, where available, it is good for all forms of sticks.

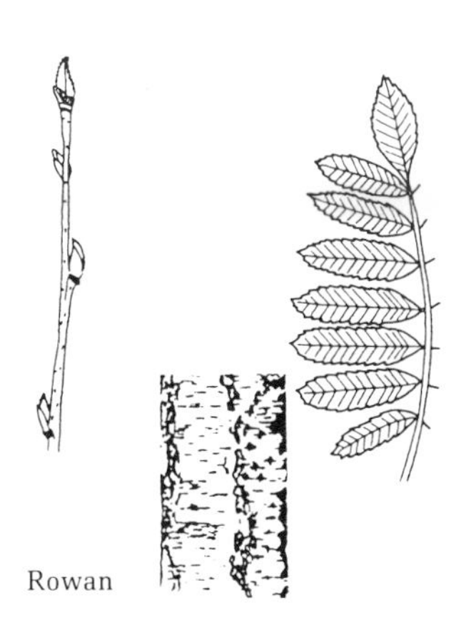

Rowan

SYCAMORE — *Acer pseudoplatanus*

This perhaps most widely found member of the maple family was introduced from France in the Middle Ages and is now widespread as a wild tree all over Britain to the point where it is almost a weed. It will grow to a height of some 100 feet, and, although it can grow to an age of 200 years, it grows quickly and can be coppiced.

The wood is creamy white, easy to work and does not warp easily. It is much used for furniture and household utensils. It is also the material most commonly used by commercial stick factories for reduced sticks.

Suckers of sycamore are far too insubstantial for making sticks. One can work them well enough but would need a very thick section before getting anything of substance.

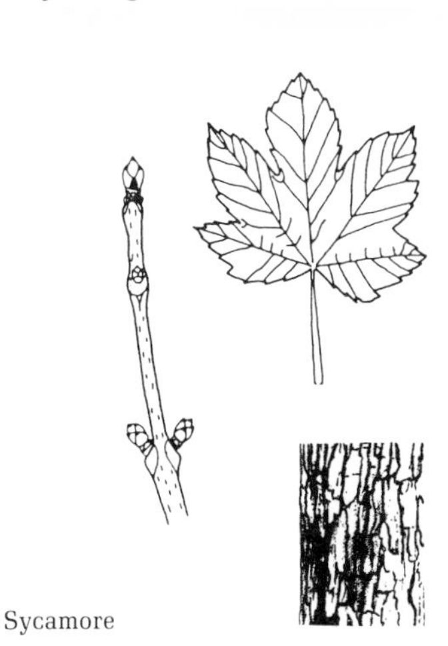

Sycamore

THISTLE

Some varieties of thistle grow to a height of six feet or more with a woody stem firm enough to make a good stick. They need only a few months' seasoning and varnishing after cleaning. There is not, as some people suppose, any need for a stiffening agent.

I have heard of stick competitions where thistle sticks were eliminated as 'not of wood'. Whilst they may not be made from a shrub or tree, the fact that they make a stick at all means that the cell structure must be woody.

The thistle, being the national emblem of Scotland, is also frequently used by stickdressers in the Borders and Lowlands as an embellishment on the nose of crooks.

GIANT THISTLE which grows to 6 ft or more can make quite good lightweight sticks.

WALNUT, EUROPEAN – *Juglans regia*

Euro' Walnut

WALNUT, BLACK – *Juglans nigra*
Walnut trees are comparatively rare and as mature trees are very valuable. It is sometimes possible to obtain from various sources offcuts large enough to carve very attractive handles.

Young growth in both forms of walnut is far too pithy to make walking sticks even after several years of growth. It can be done but not with any great satisfaction. Not even the bark gives any great effect.

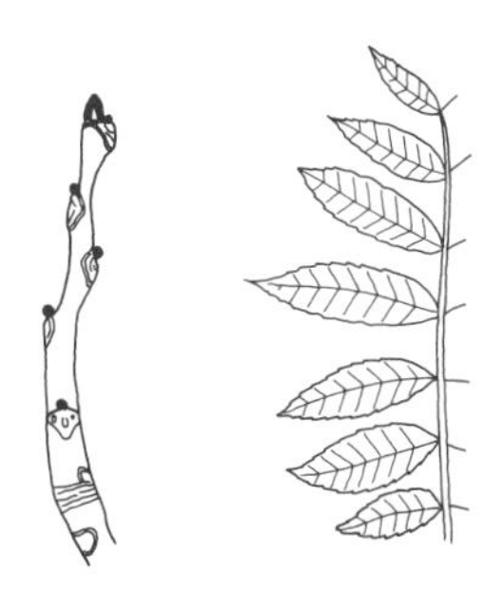

Black Walnut

WAYFARING TREE – *Viburnum lanata*
(Hoarwithy)
I have included this tree only because I could not resist doing so, on account of its name, which was given to it by the botanist Gerard. He found it growing in hedgerows along the old drove roads across the Hampshire and Surrey Downs. It is found only on chalk and limestone in southern England.

I have never heard of walking sticks made from it. The wood when green is very flexible, but there is no reason to suppose that good sticks could not be made from it after proper seasoning. The tree grows to not more than 15 feet in height and throws suckers freely.

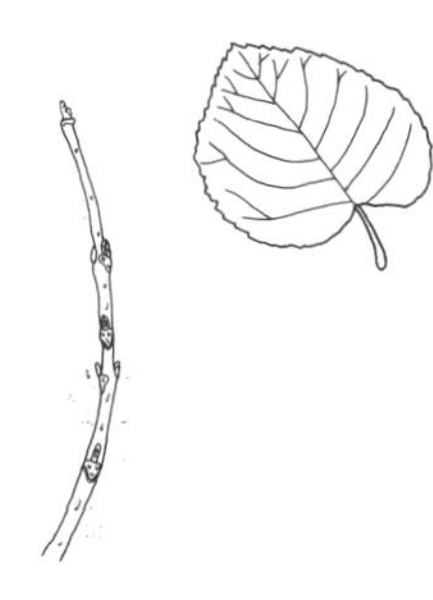

Wayfaring

WILD ROSE — *Rosa canina* etc. (Dog Rose and many others)
Over 100 species of wild rose have been identified in Britain, the dog rose being one of the best known.

The rose is of course the national flower of England and also has strong associations in folklore with summer and particularly with Midsummer Night. The wild rose is often referred to as briar. Strictly speaking briar (bruyere) — the wood best known for making pipes — actually comes from a form of tree heather growing in the Mediterranean area.

Most species of rose, including domestic varieties, are very well suited for making walking sticks with or without the bark. The thorns grow out of the bark and are difficult to retain, being very pithy inside. It is best to leave on any thorns during seasoning and then to pinch them off with flat-nose pliers.

The wood is very flexible but strong and a little heavy. When the bark is removed the wood looks almost like cane, with longitudinal fine striping. All forms of rose, however, have a strong tendency to split during seasoning where branches divide.

Wild Rose

WILLOW — *Salix sp*
Whilst it is perfectly possible to make sticks from the many species of willow, there is very little to recommend them in terms of weight or bark. There are so many other and better woods available in Britain that it is hardly worth while.

YEW — *Taxus baccata*
A native and very distinctive tree of the British Isles, the yew was of course famous in past times for providing the best wood for longbows.

This evergreen conifer is found mostly in churchyards but also elsewhere. The yew was held sacred in pagan times and is said to have provided shelter for the first Christian missionaries to Britain.

Both the bark and foliage are poisonous, as are the seeds, though not the flesh of the berries. The heartwood is a beautiful orange-brown and very durable, whilst the sapwood is nearly white, sometimes with cream-coloured inclusions.

Yew is the only conifer which does make the most excellent walking sticks. The timber can also be carved into all forms of handles and crooks. It is easy to carve but needs careful seasoning and handling. The end results are well worth the extra trouble.

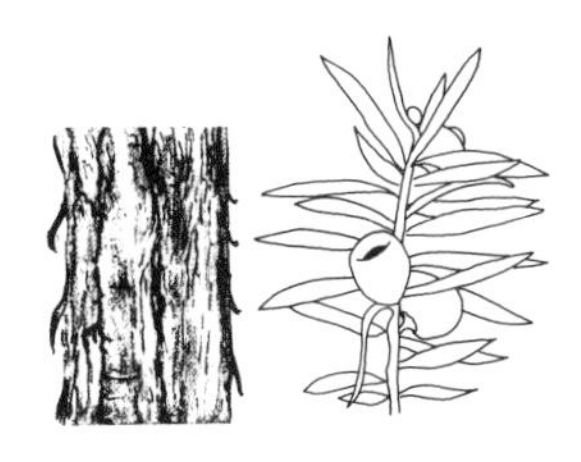

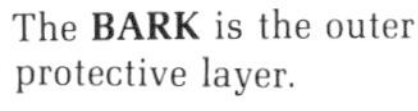

Yew

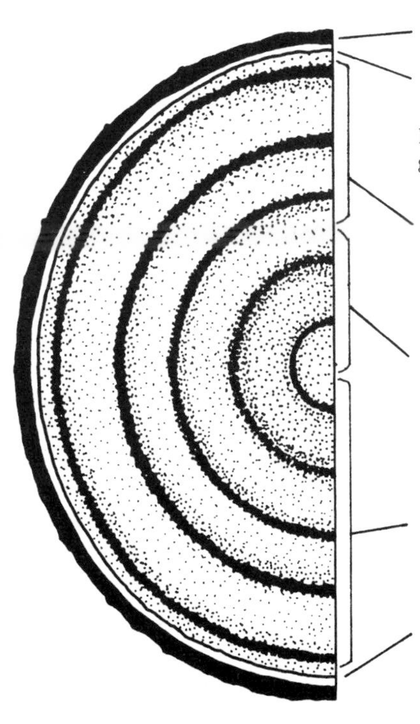

I have tried to cover most of the woods likely to be encountered by the stickmaker in Britain, both good and bad, but have had to confine myself to those found growing in the wild. Had I tried to cover all the exotic garden trees and shrubs or all the imported woods available through timber merchants I could easily have made this already long chapter into a book on its own.

Do not worry if you cannot identify a particular stick after cutting. You will learn as you go along, and one does not need to know the name of a wood to make a good stick. If it shows potential by all means cut it and have a go. If the bark does flake or wrinkle at a later stage you can always shave or peel it back to the wood. One trick if you cannot identify a wood is to bring home with you some of the twigs and put them in a vase on your mantelpiece. The buds will break into leaf fairly quickly and you can then compare them to reference books for identification.

In the long run the only way to learn your woods is to use them, get the 'feel' of them and to talk to as many knowledgeable people as will give you time.

STICKMAKING MATERIALS – EXOTIC

The following list comprises names of woods and materials which I have come across during my research into walking sticks. Some are proper names and the Latin name is given where available. Others are the pure invention of individual factories to make their products seem more exotic (castanea for sweet chestnut is one example). In other cases shippers are suspected of giving an exotic name to a material when they wanted to hide the source (Ceylon Vine appears not to originate in Ceylon and it is not at all certain that it is a vine).

Native European types of wood have been covered in a separate list.

Any suggestions, comments or additional firm data would be most gratefully received by the author c/o the publisher's address. MOST REFERENCES BELOW RELATE TO LATE 19th CENTURY.

Assyrian Thistle – from 'Smyrna'
Balow – a palm ex Singapore
Baku Cane, or Batu? *(Calamus sp.)* – viz Makore
Bamboo – *(Bambussa sp/Phyllostachys sp/Arundinaria sp)* grass family, woody stem hollow between leaf nodes. Its relative the cane has no hollows. Over 1000 species
Bamboo, Bengal
Bamboo, Japanese
Bay Tree – ex Algeria
Banana – not a tree but a herbaceous plant related to plantain
Beati *(Cassia siamea)*
Beetle Cane
Black Jack – ex South Carolina, USA, nothing else known
Black Torck – ex West Indies
Blackwood – ex Africa, can be entirely black or figured. Very similar to ebony and as dense
Bramble – ex Australia, presumably not related to European B.
Briar – *(Xanthoxylon Clara-Herculis)* ex West Indies.
Cactus
Calma Cane

Cane — applies to those semi-tropical and tropical growths which are without hollows. Most are climbing plants and grow to very great heights
Carob *(Ceratina siliqua)* the locust bean — not to be confused with Robina ex Algeria, as Caroubier.
Carolina Reed
Ceylon Vine *(? Sapindaceae)* doubtful if from Ceylon
Chi-Chi — nothing known other than one reference re sticks
Cinnamon
Coffee *(Caffea arabica)* used for sticks ex West Indies
Cork *(Quercus suber)* novelty sticks sometimes made
Crocuswood
Danta
Date Palm *(Phoenix dactylifera)* the petioles sometimes made into sticks
Devil's Walking Stick *(Aralia spinosa)* also known as Hercules' Club or Angelica Tree. Unusual native of S.E. USA. Stout upright prickly stems. Nothing else known but the name is a tantalising one for a stickmaker!
Digital Bamboo = Whangee?
Domingo
Ebony *(Diospyros ebenum)* well known
Flowered Ebony *(Brya ebenus)* ex West Indies
Eucalyptus — ex Algeria *(Eucalyptus globulus — ?)*
Gru-Gru *(Astrocaryum vulgare)* or *(Acrocomia sclarocarpa)*
Gutta Percha *(Palaquium gutta)* evergreen tree Far East
Hickory *(Carya sp.)* stated to be similar to European Ash in the properties of its wood
Ironbark — a name applied to a number of Eucalyptus species
Jambeze
Jungle (Palm)
Juniper ex Algeria
Lancewood *(Oxandra lanccolata)* ex tropical South America
Lemon Sticks *(Citrus)* much prized for their knobs
Loya ex Australia
Madagascar Bamboo
Mahadia
Malacca *(Calamus scipionum)* highly sought after
Manau *(Calamus sp)* large climbing Palm

Manilla
Marblewood — similar to ebony but figured
Marno Cane *(? Manau Cane)*
Medler ex France
Midgen Cane — type of bamboo ?
Myrtle *(Myrtus communis)* ex Algeria
Nilgheri — a jointed bamboo
Nutmeg
Olive ex Algeria
Orange *(Citrus)* very fine bark ex West Indies
Palmyra — resembles Partridge Cane in markings
Palo Diablo — very dense
Panama Cane
Partridge Cane ex China — made from a palm ?
Penang Lawyer *(Licuala ?)* from Penang
Pepper cane
Persimmon — similar to ebony
Pimento *(Pimenta officinalis)* ex West Indies & South America very hard and great favourite late 19th cent.
Pamir Vine
Pomegranate *(Punica granatum)* ex Algeria
Porcupine Wood *(Cocos nucifera)*
Quebracho — denser than water
Rajah Cane — known to come from a palm
Rattan
Rice Cane
Rock Cane
Root Rattan ex Singapore
Rosewood
Snakewood *(Piratinera guianensis)* — 'letterwood'
Soapwood *(Sapindus saponaria)* ex West Indies
Supple Jack
Tea Tree — ex China but not 'Thea'
Tobacco Plants — have been used to make sticks
Tonquin Reed — ex China
Tree Fern — said to grow on St Helena
Tree Nettle *(Celtis australis)*
Whampoa *(Phyllostachys puberula)* ex China
Whangee *(Phyllostachys nigra)* ex China
Yellow Sanders — ex West Indies
Zephyr — ex East Indies

HORN

We tend to talk about horn as if it were all one type of material when in fact it can fall into one of three very distinct categories.

1 *Compressed Hair* is, for example, what **RHINO** horn consists of. It grows from the skin and is still much sought after, not only as a supposed sexual reviver for the Chinese, but also as a symbol of manhood in some of the Arab countries where daggers with rhino horn handles are much prized. In most of Europe it is now illegal to trade even in antique rhino horn without a special licence from the Department of the Environment.

2 *Bone* is the constituent of staghorn. It is cast naturally every year and a new set of antlers grown. It cannot be

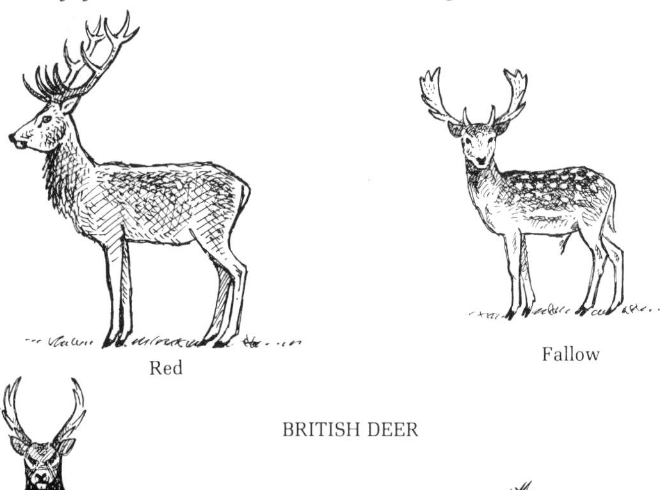

Red

Fallow

BRITISH DEER

Sika

Roe

bent by aid of heat or any other known method. Staghorn is entirely white. If one were to scrub it with soap under hot water, it would emerge as white or nearly white. The grey-to-brown colour of normal staghorn is partly dried skin and partly what the stag has rubbed off from trees and other vegetable matter.

There are six species of deer living wild in Britain. Two of these need hardly concern us much since the small **MUNTJAC** has antlers at the very most four inches long,

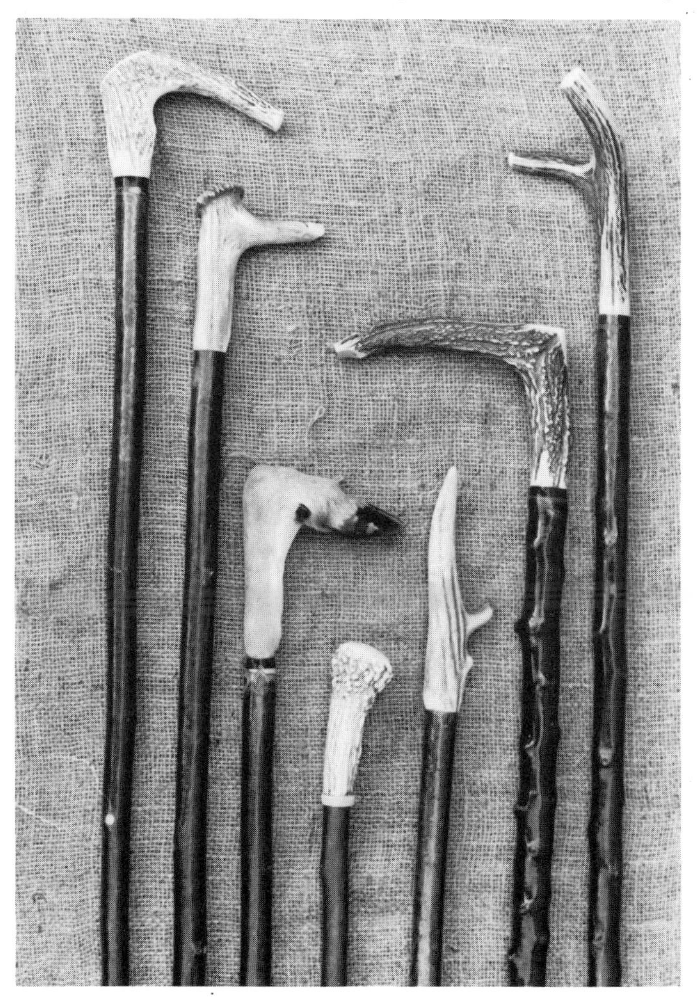

STAGHORN HANDLES with left to right: A "scrumping hook" and a whistle stick both from red deer horn, a deer foot stick, a knob stick from fallow deer, and a walker and thumbstick both made from Indian sambar horn.

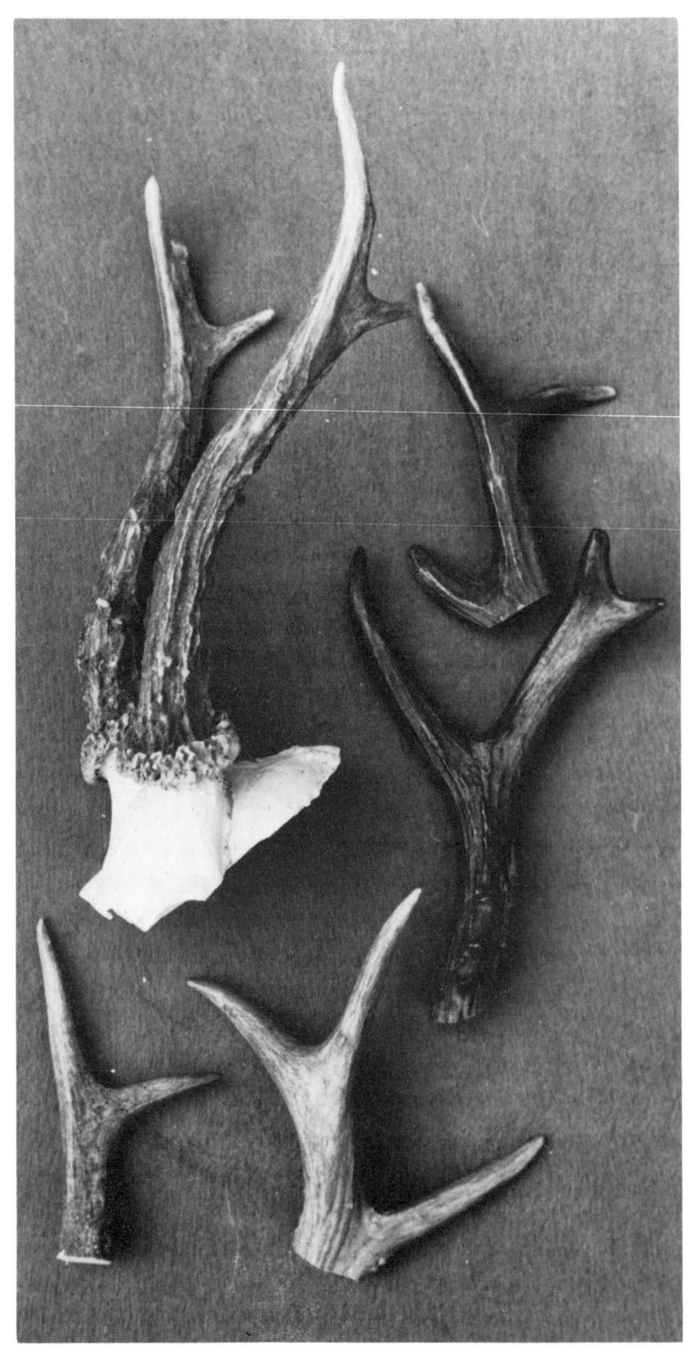

ROE DEER HORNS.

FALLOW DEER ANTLER.

and the equally small **CHINESE WATER DEER** none at all. **ROE DEER** antlers have only limited use for thumbsticks. **FALLOW DEER** give one good coronet walker handle and, usually, one thumbstick piece on each of their two antlers. The large palmated section at the top of antlers from more mature bucks is good only for snow shovels. **SIKA DEER** do not have a wide distribution in Britain but when available their antlers make good handles. This leaves the **RED DEER** for which Scotland is famous but which are also found in England and Ireland, though not in Wales. Antlers from Scottish red deer are first class for sticks, while those from further south usually tend to be too large and massive to make good handles.

It is important to realise that antlers from all European deer have a pithy centre and only staghorn from the Indian **SAMBAR DEER** has a solid white inner. This means that one cannot file too deeply into European staghorn without reaching the 'pith'.

3 *Fingernails* are the nearest comparison to the type of horn found on sheep, goat, water buffalo, ox, antelope and many more. This type of horn is most important to the stickdresser since it can be heated and bent into required shapes. It must, however, be seasoned rather like wood before it can be used satisfactorily.

RAMSHORN from various breeds of sheep. None of them are really big enough to make even a market stick.

RAMSHORN is, of course, the ideal and original material for stickdressing. It is now very difficult to obtain. Rams are not generally kept long enough to grow horns of a sufficient size and in addition there is an ever-increasing number of people interested in stickdressing.

This type of horn is not shed annually but grows a little longer each year of the animal's life from a spiky 'boss' of bone. This means that there is a resulting hollow at the base of the horn which must be trimmed off before use, as

RAMSHORN of a quality sufficient to make a good Crook.

must be any frayed part at the tip. To make a full shepherd's crook one needs about 15 to 18 inches of solid horn remaining after trimming. A market stick calls for about 12 inches of solid. Any smaller horns can always be used for practice and will usually at least make some form of walker handle. It really does pay to use inferior horns to start with to get used to working this material. If you do get hold of a good horn, you would never forgive yourself if it were ruined through inexperience.

Who knows when or where you might find another?

WATER BUFFALO horns are now extensively used for stickdressing, again as a result of the general shortage of ramshorn. Some people maintain that buffalo horn can be bent only once; not so — it can be bent as often as necessary, though it is denser and therefore a little more difficult to move than ramshorn.

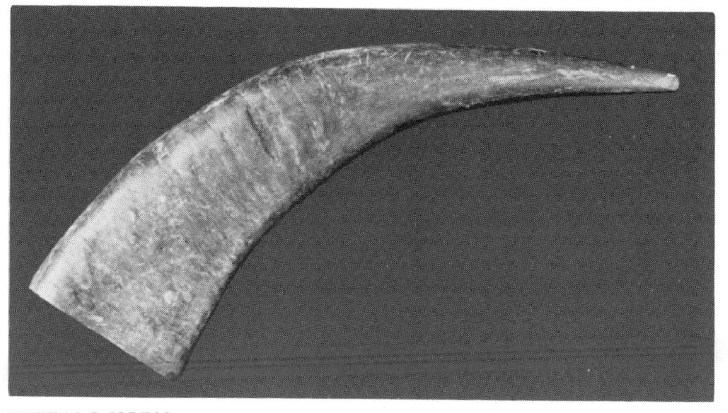

BUFFALO HORN.

Buffalo horn comes either as black (or Cape) or coloured (Siam) horn. Like everything else in life it is not quite as simple as that, and the colour of buffalo horn can vary from total jet black to a shade almost as pale as ramshorn with several colour variations in between. These range mostly from grey, through cream to almost green. They all make the most attractive crooks, even though they are not strictly the traditional material.

Other horns in this category are **GOAT**, which can be a good find but even billies are de-horned these days. If allowed to mature, they will work well.

OXHORN is equally rare these days because of the general dehorning of cattle. When available, it provides an added problem in that it does tend to delaminate very easily, and care must be taken in working with it. None the less some very good crooks have been made from oxhorn. Colours vary greatly between breeds. Most of them have what looks like a white outer skin and inside often have dark brown streaks and blotches.

A very useful source of horn material can be antique dealers and junkrooms. Even jumble sales have been known to yield big game trophies such as wild goat, antelope or the mighty kudu, but beware, as some are almost entirely hollow.

OXHORN is still plentiful. This is a shipment from abroad. It has only very limited potential for stickdressing.

CUTTING YOUR STICKS

Everything in the countryside belongs to someone – so get permission before you cut. Any farmer's or landowner's initial reaction will be, 'Leave my trees alone!' Of course stickmakers don't want large trees, we are after neglected hedges and scrubby corners – not that any farmer will admit to having any. Just ask if you can walk his hedges and copses to see if there are odd sticks you could use. Since we cut in December, January and February when the sap is down, do remember that the shooting season for most game birds does not finish until 1 February, and you must avoid any conflict or disturbance. Ideally you should get written permission to cut.

One thing I cannot teach you from the printed page is how to develop an eye for potential sticks. Keep looking and try to imagine what will make a good stick. It helps to carry with you a hooked stick exactly 36 in. long. This can be most useful in measuring a growing shank while it is still uncut. It can be most frustrating to find that a stick you have just cut is a fraction too short to use.

It is generally a waste of time to go looking in more mature woods, especially conifers, unless they are fairly open with plenty of undergrowth.

I carry the following items with me when cutting:

Saw – personally I favour a folding saw but a bow saw is as good. My own saw is the Sandvik 380. It helps if the saw frame comes to a point at one end because one can then reach into fairly tight corners.

Hedging Glove of heavy leather is useful when cutting blackthorn or gorse

Pruning Clippers are used to remove small side shoots, thus making bundling much easier. I use CEKA 5673 Ratchet Cutters as a personal preference

Ball of Twine for bundling up makes the world of difference when hauling your booty back to your vehicle

Small Trowel is very useful for digging up root handles

Close-fitting Hat – even that will be snatched off your

head at times. It helps to sew on a strap which can be tucked away inside unless needed

Waterproof Jacket with large pockets

Wellies and an **Old Pair of Trousers** are essential, since you will spend a good bit of time on your knees (apart from begging your wife's forgiveness for being late again)

Pair of Protective Glasses or Goggles – not only is blackthorn nasty stuff but even a hazel twig in the eye can be incredibly painful

First Aid Kit will almost certainly be needed at some stage

Lock- or **Sheath-knife**

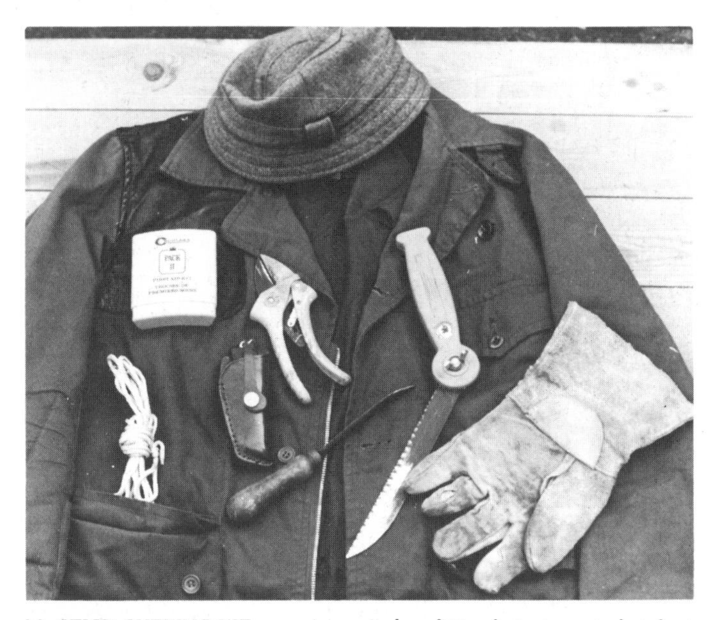

My STICK CUTTING KIT comprising: A close-fitting hat, strong jacket, first-aid kit, twine, pocket knife, ratchet cutters, folding saw, root pick and heavy hedging glove. Forgotten in the photograph but vital is a pair of protective glasses.

On reading through this list again, I'm astonished at all the items I take with me. Once packed away in a rucksack however, it won't seem so much and I can assure you that you will be thankful for every item at some stage. I usually also have a billhook in my rucksack but that really does add a lot of weight.

From bitter personal experience I strongly recommend

Neglected hedges yield good sticks.

that you buy yourself some light-coloured paint (yellow or orange is best) or even in aerosol form and apply this to the handles of your tools. It is so easy to put them down or drop them in the rough by mistake. Only when you get further on do you find that they are missing. Then to try to find your favourite saw or whatever in the undergrowth is a most frustrating experience — I know !

Once you have cut a number of sticks, bundle them up.

This is where protective glasses and probably knee pads would be essential. Despite the tangle, there are very good sticks in there.

I do this by tying them at each end and using an old leather belt between the two ties to carry the bundle slung from my shoulder. Beware of blackthorn and hawthorn spines which can badly damage the bark of other sticks when bundled tight. I trim branches and spines back to about $\frac{1}{2}$ in. in length.

A typical patchy bank full of stick cutting potential.

Flowering Blackthorn in late March to early April can be recognised and marked by their mass of white flowers.

It pays not to leave rubbish after cutting. We don't want to get ourselves a bad name and it takes only a couple of minutes to push offcuts back into the hedge.

Remember with blackthorn, if the soil allows, to dig down to the root system as in most cases you will find a perfect cross handle already formed because of the habit of blackthorn's freely throwing suckers well out on the roots.

SEASONING

> When's the best time to cut a stick?
> 'When thou sees the blighter —
> Afore ought else 'as 'im.'

Despite that, the best time to cut a stick is when the sap is down during December, January and February. Even then the moisture content can be very high and if seasoning is not done carefully checks and cracks can develop.

Seasoning should not be hurried — the general rule of thumb for all timber is a year per inch of thickness. It is best to keep all stick shanks for a full year before working on them anyway.

If cutting outside the optimum time cannot be avoided then it should be done after the period of maximum sap flow (March to July) and when growth has started to slow down between August and November. If it proves necessary to cut at this time, then seasoning must be done with even greater care in order to slow down as much as possible the rate at which moisture leaves the wood.

There is always an exception to every rule. It is very difficult to keep the bark on holly and oak. For the latter it is hardly worth while since it is not very attractive. Holly bark on the other hand, can be quite attractive, and one way of greatly increasing the chances of its shrinking on tight during seasoning is to varnish it the same week as it is cut, having first scrubbed off all dirt and algae.

Initially all cut material should be left out of doors but under cover from rain. Stacking bundles vertically will speed up the drying process, stacking horizontally will slow it down. Wind can also be a critical factor and if drying out is too fast, stresses will be caused on the outside of the wood leading to cracks. It may seem almost unbelievable but seasoning of some timber requires water to be sprayed on to it to allow even drying.

Only after the wood has been out of doors for some six to nine months should bringing it indoors into an unheated workshop be considered. Even then, avoid extreme heat such as boiler rooms or centrally heated houses. Stacking wood on the rafters in the garage can cause considerable damage to the wood as a lot of heat can be trapped there on hot sunny days.

Even if it is planned to remove the bark eventually, this should on no account be done before seasoning is complete since in most woods it will lead to cracks.

I bundle my sticks with string after cutting. This not only makes transporting them very much easier but also they can be left in the bundle during seasoning. Originally I used to seal the end of each stick with paint to prevent splitting but found this rather time consuming. Now I simply cut my sticks slightly overlength and trim away the inch or so which may have split.

Experiments are still in progress on an alternative method of seasoning which may allow closer control of the moisture loss rate through the bark. So little is known about the seasoning factors of various types of wood used in stickmaking that the field is wide open for further tests. Meanwhile the rule of thumb must be 'a year an inch' but if in doubt – wait. It can be fatal if you bring that special stick you found straight into the house, particularly with the fierce central heating most of us have now.

You can still admire, finger and even dream of that special stick by placing it, say, just inside your workshop door or in the garage lying flat on the concrete.This then allows you to pick it up whenever you think of it, tweak it across your knee to straighten it and think of what a fine stick it will make. At the first tweak the green wood will go right back to its original shape but gradually, as you continue to tweak it across your knee as you think of it in passing, it will become straighter than any that has been steamed.

Much has been heard lately about the use of PEG. Polyethylene Glycol is a water-soluble wax used commercially for the fast seasoning of green wood by soaking so that the wax replaces the water in the wood cells. It would seem to have little application in stickmaking because it is very difficult to apply any sort of varnish over PEG. If left without a totally waterproof finish, any wood will become moist on damp days. PEG is also very expensive and one might do better by spending the cash on some special exotic wood.

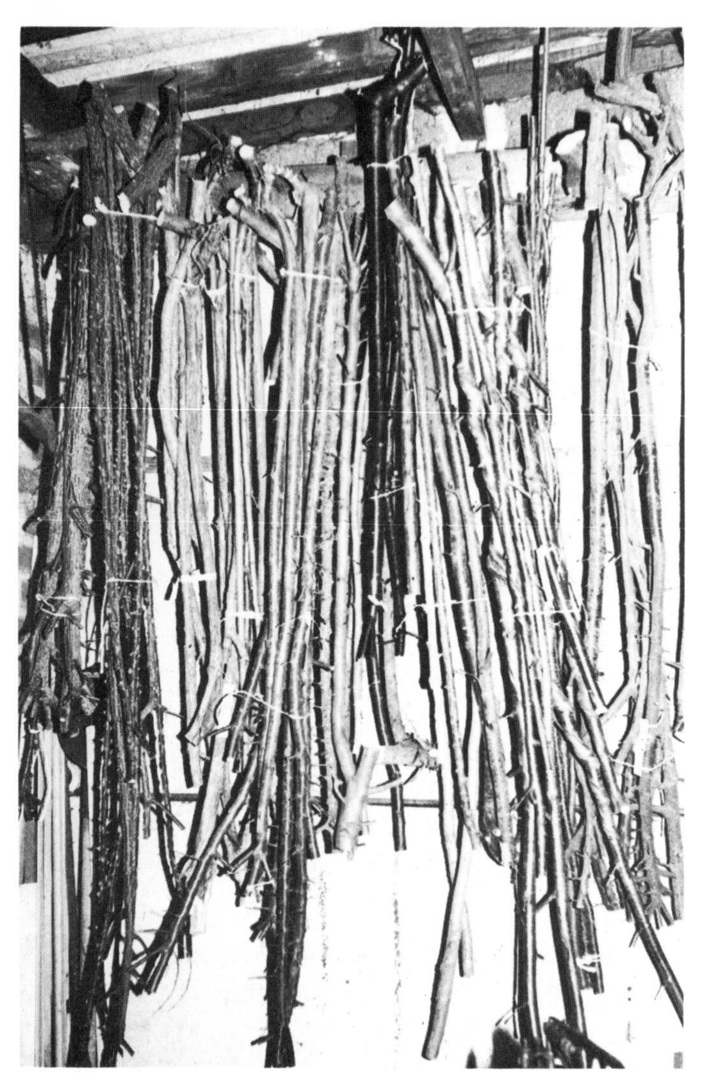

Cut sticks hanging up in bundles for seasoning.

STRAIGHTENING SHANKS

After patiently seasoning your shanks for 12 months comes the exciting time to go and see what you put away the year before. Then follows the straightening over steam. There is no point in trying to steam green wood as it will simply revert to its original shape.

Complicated steam boxes are quite unnecessary but a design for one is given here for those who would prefer to use one. They will certainly need one if they wish to bend handles on to sticks.

An electric kettle on a workmate with a rack over it is all that is needed for steaming sticks straight. The illustration shows the idea of a rack to hold three or four sticks at a time over the steam, covered with sacking, with other sticks above already sorted out as the next batch. The sacking is there to hold the steam to the wood and make the heat penetrate better. The kettle is the type which continues boiling but throws out the plug only when it has nearly boiled dry.

A simple but very effective steaming set-up consisting of an ordinary kettle, and a rack clamped in a B & D Workmate. The upper rungs in the rack are only for presorting the shafts.

It is best to work the middle of the stick first — leave it to set/cool whilst working on other sticks — then work on each end section in turn with a cooling period in between.

Once the wood has been steamed long enough, take out one shank at a time and flex it across the knee slightly beyond the point to which it is intended to bend it. Lean it lightly against a wall to cool off. Carry on with the next one.

Some woods are difficult to move, as are the thicker ones on occasion. These are best clamped (after steaming) in the jaws of the workmate using corks on the pressure points (*see* illustration). Even the thickest wood will have set well within a few hours. The corks, which tend to get squashed rather flat after a while, can easily be rejuvenated by boiling in water for a short time and letting them dry out.

A Method of Clamping to Straighten After Steaming.

The horse is an old and well-tried piece of equipment for straightening shanks. It consists of a heavy two-inch board about 12 inches wide and some 50 inches long. This is propped up at an angle of approximately 60 degrees to the horizontal by a strut at the back. Notches of varying sizes cut into each edge provide the leverage points for straightening bends in shanks.

A modern version of the horse is the straightening post illustrated, which must be made as robust as possible to withstand the very considerable forces exerted by levering.

Easy to bend are: Hazel, Ash, Sweet Chestnut, Rowan, Holly and, particularly, Blackthorn. A little more difficult are: Cherry, Birch, Broom and Oak. The ones that have caused me the most headaches are Yew and Gorse. Even so, the last two are among the most rewarding.

Finally, a decisive advantage of the steam method of straightening is that some sticks will revert after some months to their original cast — even long after they have been made into finished sticks. This method allows them to be straightened even through the finish coat of varnish.

The method described is definitely not the traditional one used in an attempt in the North. They straighten over a naked flame, though sometimes metal foil is wrapped round the bark by stickdressers to protect it. However, it needs only a brief moment of distraction and the bark can be irretrievably scorched. Nothing can put that right other than stripping the bark altogether. Steam, on the other hand, can be left playing on the bark almost indefinitely without causing any damage.

TO BARK or NOT

The final appearance of a stick can be made to vary depending on which of the four basic ways of making it has been used:

1 With the bark left on – This requires a well-seasoned bark which has shrunk tight to the wood. If it is wrinkled, the chances are that it will begin to flake when used and look unsightly. A few woods such as hawthorn, gorse, sweet chestnut and some others have a bark which does not appeal to me at all and I always use one of the other three methods. Among the very best bark you can count blackthorn, broom and cherry.

Privet, oak and holly present particular problems since it is difficult in most cases to retain the bark. There is a way of improving your chances with holly and privet by varnishing the sticks completely within days of cutting them, but this means that they will take twice as long to season since we are slowing down the rate of evaporation of moisture.

All that is required in the actual preparation of the stick prior to applying a finish of varnish or oil, is to scrub the bark clean of algae and to dry it.

2 Bark stripped off – Never should the bark be stripped before seasoning is complete or most woods will begin to split.

I find the best way to strip the bark is to cut away the outer layer with not too sharp a knife taking care not to go too deep. A few hours' soaking either in the bath (if you can keep the family at bay) or in the fishpond will soften the underbark, and it can be easily scraped off with your blunt knife or even fingernails. You may have to repeat the soaking for a final clean up.

Of course, once the bark has been removed the wood itself appears rather pale. That can look quite good left as it is, but it is more usual to tone down or stain the wood in some way (*see* Staining and Fuming).

3 Shaved or 'Reduced' – These two methods are grouped together as in both cases we cut into the actual wood. The best tool for shaving a stick is the Surform 21-215 Shaver although those who have the facility could also use a shavehorse and drawknife. Other Surform types will not do as they have different cutters.

To turn a stick of 36 in. by less than 1 in. diameter on a lathe is an undertaking which only two people I know will attempt. The problem is 'whip' on the thin length of wood even with steadies. The traditional and much more reliable way is to 'reduce' sticks using two special tools known as traps and frazes. The thick end of the shank is held in a special chuck rotating quite slowly (say about 200 to 300 rpm). The other end rotates free. The fraze is something like a giant pencil sharpener and is used first to round off the wood to reduce it to a regular diameter along its entire length. Following this the trap is used.

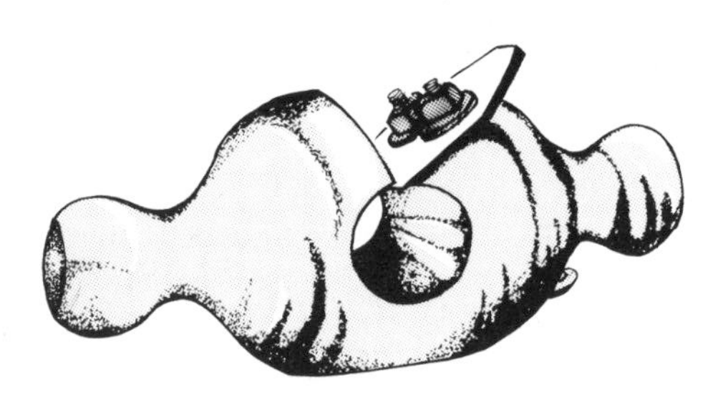

A traditional "Fraze" – for rounding a square section of wood as the first stage in making a rounded (so-called "reduced") shaft.

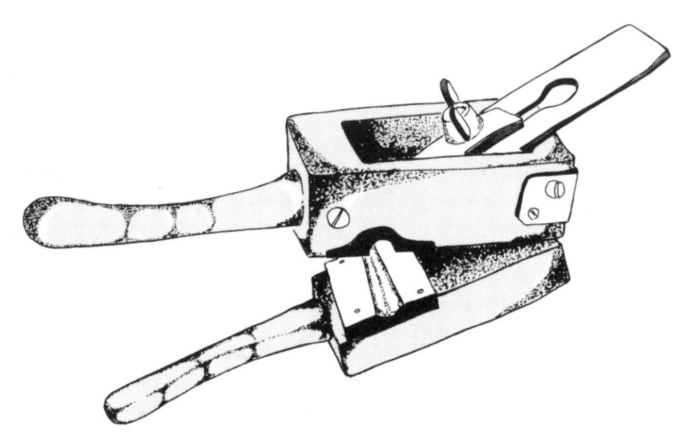

A traditional "Trap" – a rounding plane which allows for the cutting of a taper along a "reduced" shaft.

The metal equivalent of a trap for tapering shafts.

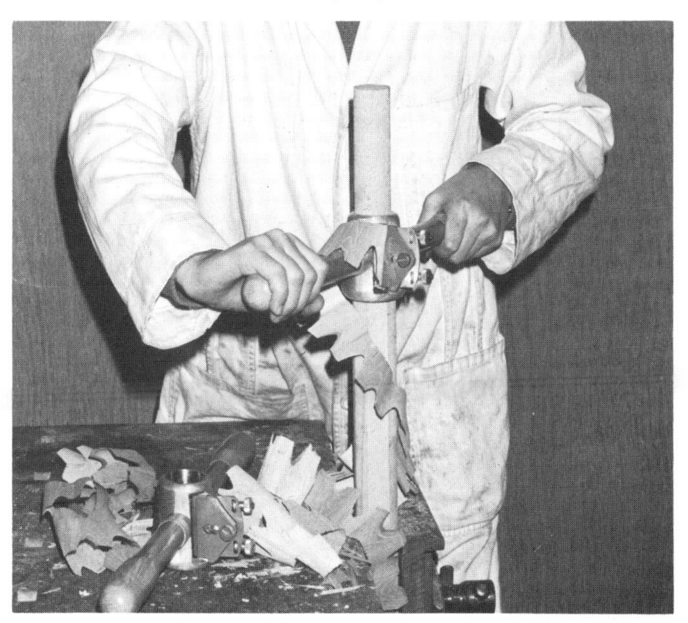

A modern aluminium rounder plane (fraze) developed by Mr. F. Lambert and now manufactured to his design by Ashem Crafts.

This consists of a plane with a hinged bottom plate. There is a handle on each section, both facing the same way. The trap is started at the chuck end and, while moving it along the wood towards the free end, the handles are slowly squeezed together thus forming the taper.

Traps and frazes are now available in cast metal from Ashem Crafts, 2 Oakleigh Avenue, Hallow, Worcester WR2 6NG. These were developed over a period of some 25 years by Fred Lambert, and their manufacture has at last been taken up by Ashem Crafts. I have made some very fine reduced shafts with these tools, although their prime application is in chair-making.

Certain woods look particularly splendid when reduced or shaved and then lightly stained. Fuming also works well. The more knobs and bumps on the stick before reducing the better because the year-rings in the wood take more staining thus producing a beautiful watermark-like effect.

Blackthorn, hawthorn and holly respond particularly well to this treatment.

4 Underbark – This is possibly the most unusual method of making a stick. In fact I don't know anyone else who uses it but it is nevertheless very rewarding. Hawthorn has a bark which I find disappointing and yet the underbark has a lovely light-brown fibrous texture. By careful sanding away of the outer bark this can be exposed. When treated with boiled linseed oil the underbark really comes to life.

This method also works well on rhododendron when you can find unbranched sections of sufficient length. Experiments will probably produce other woods on which this treatment is beneficial.

STAINING and FUMING

STAINING

This may be required when a stick has been peeled, reduced or shaved to tone down the colóur of the natural pale wood. There are many good brands of stain available, but experimentation is needed to ensure that the stain used is compatible with the varnish used to finish the stick. Combined staining varnishes are also available which can be useful on sticks made from such woods as gorse. They do not penetrate too deeply and can be wiped over with a clean rag before they have dried off, thus leaving the stain only in the natural deep fissures giving the stick the immediate appearance of old age. The antique trade knows all about this trick, and in certain cases it can look most effective. Certain suppliers now sell stains in felt-tip pens. These can be immensely useful in toning down any glaring pale blazes on bark sticks after the removal of side branches. Although not strictly a stain, I have even seen soot rubbed into peeled holly giving it a highly attractive granular grey. Experimentation is the order of the day, or week!

The steaming of carved handles can greatly enhance them. For example, a particular dog's markings can be applied to a carving of it. One idea which worked particularly well was to carve a duck, not as the usual head alone, but as a full-bodied duck to a much smaller scale. The pale bill and body markings were then painted on in clear varnish and, once this had dried, a walnut stain was applied all over. Of course the stain did not take on the varnished sections, giving a very good contrast. A further bonus effect was that since the duck had been carved with the grain running from head to tail, more stain was taken up on the end grain thus giving slightly darker areas on the breast and tail.

FUMING

This is a technique of colouring wood, usually over ammonia fumes. The method is easy, can hardly go wrong and produces first-rate results. The only disadvantage is that if you are not careful the ammonia can produce tears – or worse effects if one is downright negligent.

The method involves keeping all the bark scrapings from peeling and infusing these, together with any left-over tea bags, with boiling water — just like making tea. The resulting brew is then wiped, hot or cold, on to the wood with a piece of foam sponge. The well-saturated wood is then hung in a plastic gutter pipe with a container with a small amount of strong ammonia below it. A plastic bag over the top will be sufficient as a lid. The process works best in warmer weather when the ammonia can vaporise well, but your family definitely will not thank you if you try this indoors. One major advantage of this method over staining is that there is no problem of streaking, and by checking every few hours you can decide how deep you want the colour to be.

Like all woodwork, one has to develop a 'feel' for the method and do tests to find out more on the effect on various woods. You can also go on and try variations on this theme. For example, I have found that crushed oak-apples work well when added to the brew. A slightly redder colour is obtained by treating the wood with a solution of three-quarters of an ounce of pyrogallic acid in a quart of water before applying the brew. I have not yet experimented with pyrogallic acid actually added to the brew.

The result of fuming can be spectacular on some woods such as blackthorn (if you can bring yourself to peel it), hawthorn, rowan and oak. Wild rose seems to swell up, often causing shakes, so care is needed.

When first removed from the fuming chamber, the wood will look rather disappointing, dull and a little darker than when finished as it will still be wet. Dry it out completely, sand down the whiskers which will have been raised by the moisture and apply boiled linseed oil. When rubbed down with very fine wire wool such as '000' or '0000' the final colour will appear. This, you will find, goes quite a depth into the wood allowing minor corrections without exposing bare pale wood.

The best ammonia to use is so-called 8-80 which will probably have to be specially ordered by your chemist. Ordinary household ammonia will also do the job, only more slowly.

BENDING HANDLES

Handles on 'crook walkers' are traditionally made by steaming the shanks in hot damp sand. The modern stickmaker has the choice of making himself a traditional steaming oven as illustrated or a steambox which also has several other applications. A kettle will not do here, since we need to heat some 15 in. of wood on the end of the stick and a kettle will cover only about 4 to 5 in.

A steaming oven can be constructed quite simply out of bricks, with a steel tray on top having a lip of about six inches and being filled with sand. Reinforcing rods under will be essential as this amount of sand weighs a great deal even before it is damped with water.

On the other hand, a steambox is much more mobile, easier to make and has many more applications. Steamboxes can be constructed in many ways – some good ones are shown in Jack Hill's *A Complete Practical Book of Country Crafts* – and we show one design here.

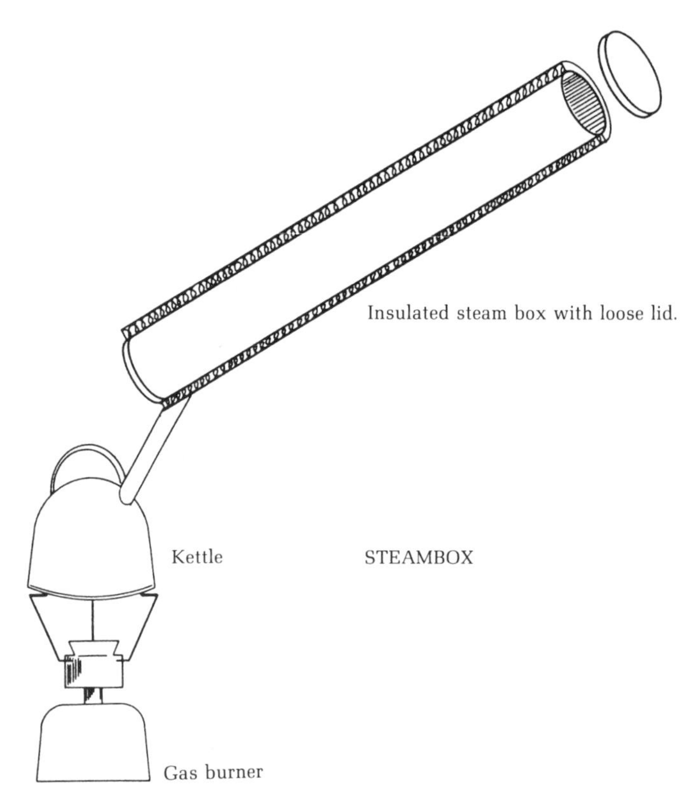

STEAMBOX

Important factors are :

i Steam can be highly dangerous, and blocked tubes and the like can lead to devastating explosions. It is also, by definition, very hot and can cause bad scalds to the unwary
ii The source of heat can be a kettle element, gas burner or a conventional wood fire
iii The box can be of wood, elm being very good, or metal. The temptation to use large plastic pipes such as soil pipes should be resisted. Even the heaviest will go soft in the steam and bend into useless shapes. Corrugated

flue liners may seem a good idea but the corrugations make it very difficult to slide the sticks down them. The box must, of course, be long and wide enough to take a reasonable number of shanks at a time

iv The supports for the box must be firm and ideally should hold the box on quite a pronounced slope so that condensed water can be drained back into the boiler

v All joints in piping should only be a loose fit to avoid the build up of pressure in the event of blockages elsewhere

BOILING for HANDLE BENDING.

To prepare for steaming the handles into a crook shape you require shanks at least 44 in. (112 cm) long, with a notch cut about half an inch from the thick end. A 12-in. length of string should be tied in the middle onto this notch with the two long tails of string hanging free. Remember to prepare only as many shanks as you have bending rolls available.

Trial and error will give the exact time required for steaming. It is almost impossible to give accurate figures since they vary with method, wood types and thicknesses. Insufficient steaming will lead to cracking during bending, while over-steaming will cause wrinkling on the inside of the bent handle but will do no permanent damage to the wood.

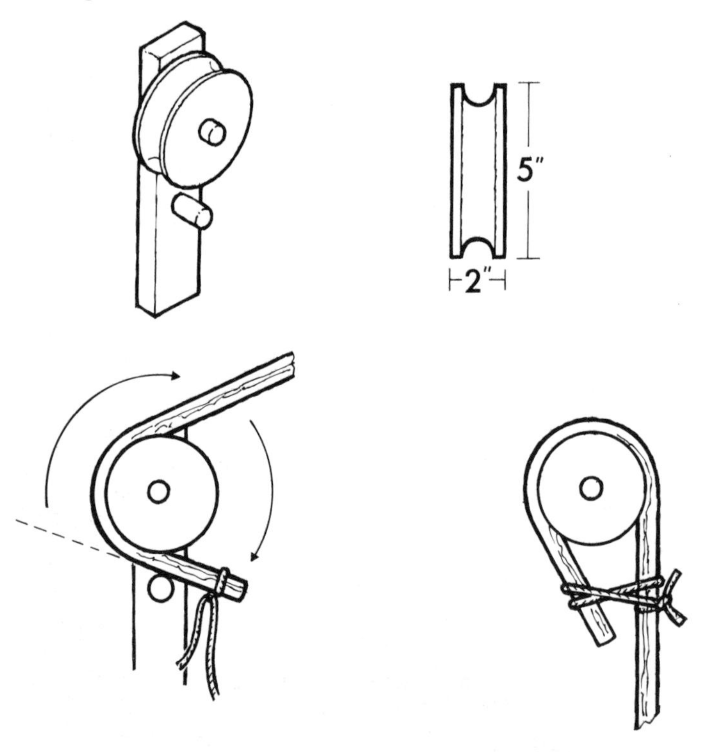

The bending rolls should be drilled out to a size that will loosely fit the fixing bolt used to bolt them to a very sturdy beam (min. 3 x 5 in.). A wing-nut is used to hold them in place. The beam itself should be securely held in a vice, alternatively clamped or bolted to a sturdy bench.

Make sure, however, that you have a clear swing in your workshop for the stick when this is taken around in the bending. Close to the bending roll and strongly fixed to the beam should be a firm stop against which the notch of the steamed shank is set and the stick then eased round the bending roll. At this stage, quite a few sticks will look as if they have gone badly wrong in that slivers of wood will have sprung loose at the top of the curve. Not to worry, this can be sorted out at a later stage. Tie the two ends of the string tightly round the shank as close as possible to the notched nose. The wood will spring back somewhat once the string is removed. But for now, take

BENT HANDLE SETTING ON ROLL.

the stick, complete with its bending roll, from the board and hang it away somewhere warm to set. Some hours later cut the string and pull out the roll from inside the bent handle. This will be stiff, but it should be possible to achieve this against the spring of the wood. It was about 1865 that a certain Mr William Dangerfield of Gloucestershire discovered that it helps to play a flame quickly over the handle to set the bend even more firmly. This should be done with care to avoid scorch. Modern technology has come to our assistance in the form of the Black and Decker paint-stripper gun, which seems to be equally effective and works at the touch of a button.

Now, back to those sticks which split across the top of the curve. Carefully shave away the splinters, removing all loose fibres, while remembering to cut with the grain. This, followed by sandpaper and varnish, will give you a very serviceable 'polished top' walking stick.

CARVING

Whether you are carving simple wooden crooks or more detailed items, you need first to lay out your shape. This is best done by tracing your shape onto a sheet of rigid clear plastic such as Perspex, and then cutting your template from this. When you lay this onto your piece of wood, you can see through to any faults in the wood so that you can avoid them and can also allow for grain direction. Once your positioning is decided, trace round the outside of the template.

On shepherds' crooks and other handle shapes this is sufficient, but on some other carvings you will need to trace the outlines for the other two dimensions.

The next step is to cut these outlines either with a bandsaw (if you have one) or a coping saw. I find it a great help to glue back my offcuts with double-sided tape until all the cutting out is complete. By gluing back my off-cuts

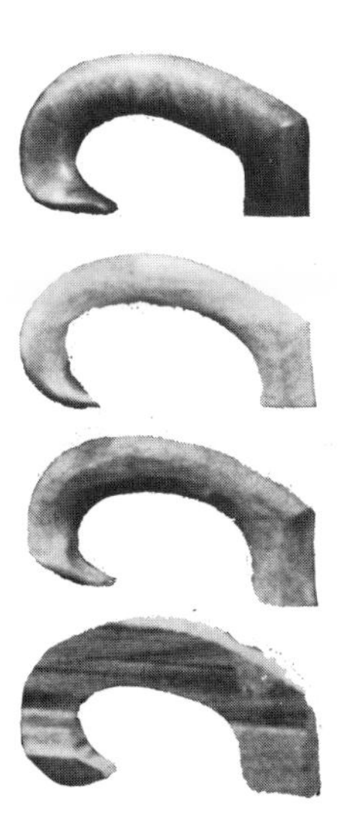

The Four Stages in Carving A Handle. Starting at the bottom: 1. Rough Blank cut out with a saw; 2. Carved with a Stanley knife; 3. Sanded smooth and finally 4. Varnished.

KNIFE CARVING

These pictures show the four cuts and holds which are not only safer but also require considerably less effort. They show the holds for a right-handed carver and should be reversed for left-hand work.
Most beginners attempt carving by holding the wood in one hand and making sweeping away cuts with the other. This results in a wild swing of the knife. Not only is this much more dangerous but also requires considerably more effort and should generally be avoided. It is also much more difficult to do accurate work this way.

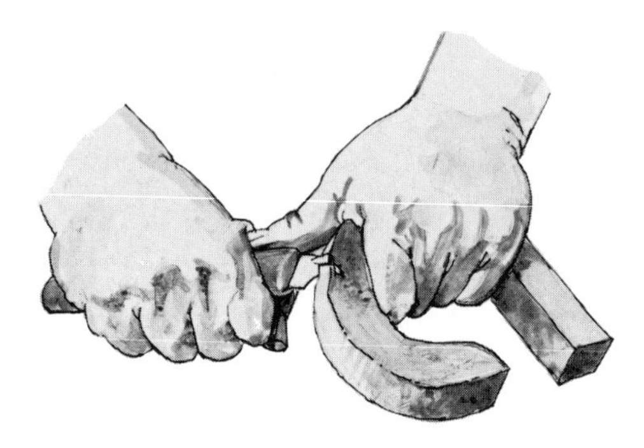

A. THUMBPUSH – this is the most commonly used handhold for carving with a knife. The wood is held by the four left fingers leaving the left thumb free to prop the top of the knife handle (but NOT the back of the blade). A cutting action is achieved by levering the knife against the left thumb.

B. BACKPULL – this is often needed when the run of the grain makes the thumbpush cut impossible. It consists of using the left thumb as a backstop at the top of the knife handle so that if the knife slips out of the wood, it will be stopped short.

C. THUMBPULL – this method involves cutting towards yourself using short strokes. The left thumb is braced against the back of the wood. Take care not to let the thumb project into the line of cut in case the knife slips.

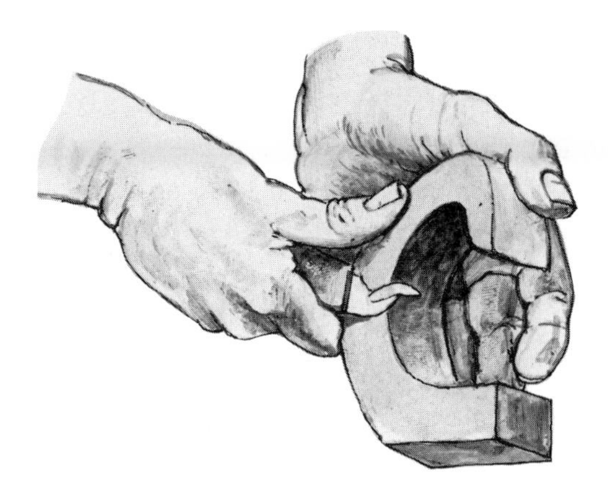

D. DRAWPULL – this cut is the most appropriate when carving on the inside of a curve. It is a sweeping cut guided by the right thumb. The work is held by all five fingers on the left hand.

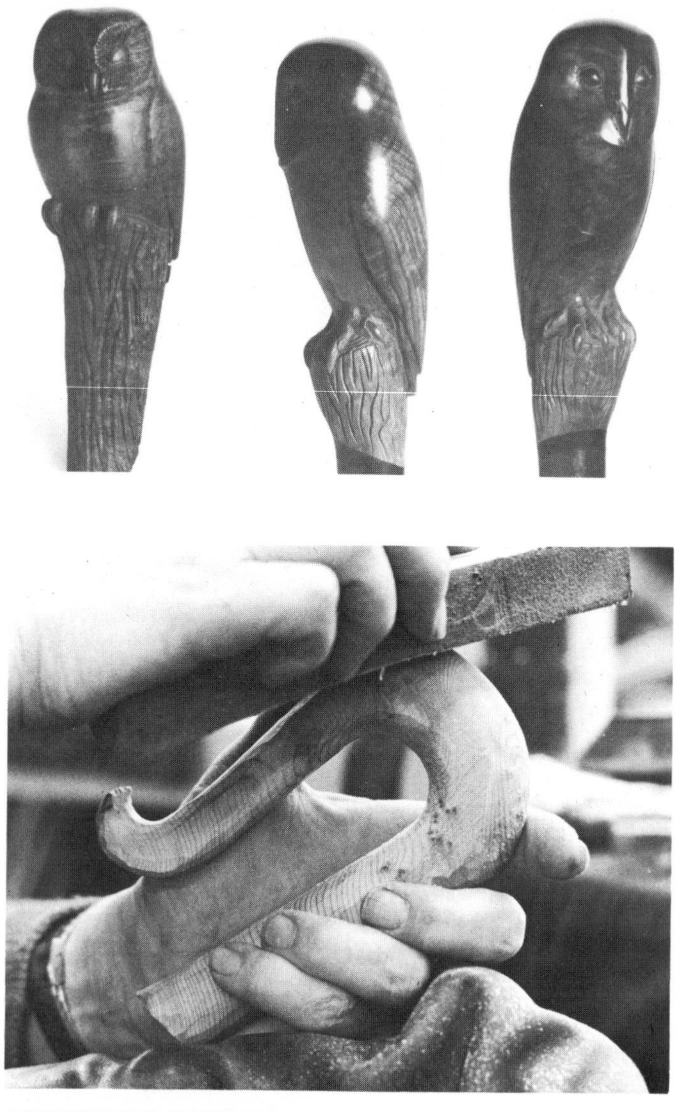

A WOODEN LEG CROOK IN THE MAKING.

the block will remain square and therefore easier to saw. All the bits can then easily be prised loose, leaving only your roughed-out carvings.

The cardinal rule for carving wood is to cut with or across the grain but never against it. Go by touch! If you feel the knife or chisel start to dig in, turn the tool or the wood round and cut in the other direction. Forcing it will only make matters worse and leave torn fibres which can be very difficult to remove later.

Try to keep control of your tools at all times. Sweeping cuts should always be away from you and are best avoided anyway. All cuts should be made in such a way that if the blade does slip it cannot cut you, or others. It helps if you develop a technique of bracing your cutting tool with the thumb of the non-cutting hand.

I am myself totally against the use of rasps for the fast removal of wood on a carving. They leave deep grooves which can be remarkably difficult to remove during the finishing stages. It almost seems as if rasps bruise the deeper layers of wood.

TOM HANSON, a woodcarver of very considerable talent with a true love and understanding of wood. Seen here instructing on one of the many stickmaking courses that he and the author run in various parts of Britain.

Working only with sharp tools is not just a fad, neither is it a waste of time. Sharp tools save time, by cutting faster and more accurately. They are also safer because less force is required. If you are using Stanley knives change the blade frequently, with chisels, hone them regularly before they become noticeably blunt.

To sharpen a carving chisel correctly you require a very fine stone such as the Hard Black Arkansas, which is an expensive item but one which should last a lifetime. Never use the stone without a coating of light oil as a lubricant. The sharpening of any cutting tool involves wearing away metal until a very fine burr of metal is produced along the entire length of the edge. The finer the stone used, the finer this burr or thin wire of metal will be and consequently the better will be the cutting edge. Further sharpening on the stone or on a strop will cause this fine wire of steel to break off leaving a good edge.

Honing is always done with the edge set at the correct angle, usually about 20 degrees, and by pushing the edge into the direction of honing. Since both hands are needed for this to be done correctly, the stone is best fixed down firmly. Stropping works in the reverse in that the edge is trailed to prevent it from cutting into the rather softer surface of the strop.

This is easily made from a length of old leather belt with the fuzzy side up onto which one rubs a mixture of tripoli or jewellers' rouge and any light oil. My own is fixed to a length of plywood making it even easier to use.

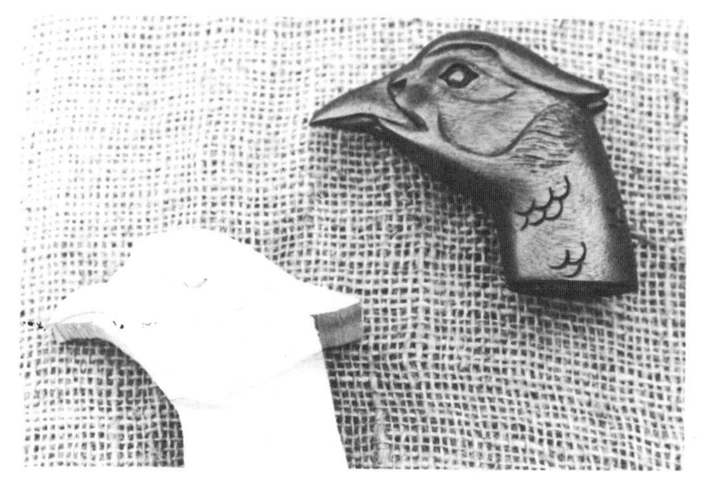

Detailed figure carving is beyond the scope of this book and I would rather refer you to the excellent book by David Orchard listed in the Bibliography. The carving of handles and crooks is a matter of gradually reducing the square or rectangular cross-section of the roughed-out blank to an even curve all round without any flat sides. Your tool is bound to leave small flat spots which will be sanded away later, but you should aim to have the overall shape as rounded as possible. The thumb of the non-cutting hand is invaluable for feeling the shape as you go along.

Once you are satisfied that the shape cannot be improved, start by sanding with 60- or 80-grit sandpaper. I use cloth-backed material when I can get it and staple it to a piece of 2 x 1 batten and in between I sandwich a layer of hard foam. This makes an excellent sanding tool which is firm and yet will follow curves. With this remove all the small ridges and flats left by your cutting tool.

This is followed by the second sanding stage with 120- or 160-grit. The lower the grit number the coarser the

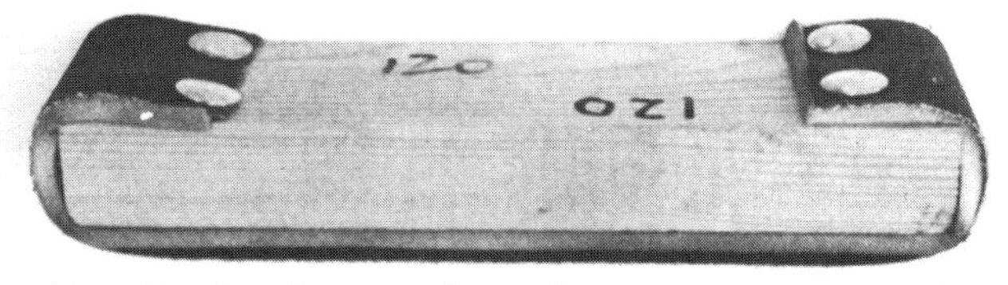

sanding. For harder woods such as yew use 60- and then 100-grit, and for softer woods 80- and then 120- or even 160-grit. This second sanding, again with pads, should remove all the scratches from the previous coarse sanding. Rub only with the grain. Double check at every stage that you have left no rough patches. It is quite surprising how you can think a sanding stage is complete until you see the piece in sunlight, usually the next morning.

If you are satisfied with your sanding, apply boiled linseed oil liberally by hand. If you can keep a few ounces of oil in a wide-neck and airtight jar, you can dip your fingers into it and then work the oil well into the wood with your palm. Never use natural linseed oil since it contains impurities which prevent it from setting hard (oxidising). After leaving the boiled linseed oil for a while to soak in, wipe away any oil left on the surface.

Should you at this stage discover that there are scratch marks still visible, don't use sandpaper as this will clog in no time with oil. Use '0' steel wool followed by '000' or '0000', then re-oil, wipe and as they say 'proceed to the next stage', which consists of rubbing down the linseed oil with 600-grit wet and dry paper. The resulting oil and wood sludge should be worked well into the grain thus sealing it. The boiled linseed finish is not fully waterproof, at best it can be described as 'showerproof'. A further form of finish will be needed for waterproofing.

Basic carving tools

1 x Stanley knife type 99 or 99E with sliding blade to take many Stanley straight blades type 1992
1 x Stanley knife type 99 or 99E with sliding blade to take many Stanley curved trimmer blades 5192
1 x Stanley knife type 00 (this is a slim yellow knife held together by a large black screw)
Many Stanley blades type 5901
1 set of 5 or 6 palm chisels

"It's easy, just remove the bits that don't look like a duck!"

STICKDRESSING

A horn of considerable size is required for 'dressing' a crook. Ramshorn is the most desirable but water buffalo is now often used, and even goatshorn makes a good dressed stick. Oxhorn on the other hand is generally rather brittle and usually has insufficient solid material. All these horns grow on a projection of bone from the skull, therefore bearing a large hollow section. Only the solid horn and some of the hollow is usable. For example some 15-18 in. of good horn is required for a neck crook, 12-15 in. For a leg cleek or market stick and anything less than that may only make a walking stick handle. Any hollow part should have a wall thickness of at least $\frac{3}{8}$ in. all round or there will not be enough material to bulk up for the neck of the handle.

The age of the horn and the environment in which the animal grew up will have a distinct bearing on the hardness of the horn when worked. The longer it has been seasoned after the ram's demise the harder it will be, and the easier the life of the ram the softer it will be.

Tools required

1 ea	Large Vice (with jaws at least 4 in. deep vertically)
2 ea	Steel or Hardwood Plates 6 × 8 × $\frac{1}{2}$ in.
1 ea	Steel or Hardwood Plates 6 × 12 × $\frac{1}{2}$ in. (4 in. of one corner removed to level of the vice jaw)
1	4-in. length of 1–1$\frac{1}{2}$ in. I/D pipe cut vertically in half
1 ea	Bucket or Tub of cold water
1 ea	Mist/spray Plastic Bottle
	Wood Wedges
1 ea	Gas Blowtorch
1 ea	Can of Light Oil and Brush
1 ea	2-in. and 1$\frac{1}{4}$ in.-dia. Round Posts in steel or hardwood
1 ea	18-in. Sash Cramp

1 ea Half-round Rasp $\frac{3}{4}$–1 in. wide
1 ea Round Rasp $\frac{1}{2}$ in. dia.
Several Wood Blocks for setting the shape of the grip line and nose

*The plates should be fitted loosely to the vice jaws so that they 'self-adjust' for differences in taper of the various parts of the crook.

The making of a horn handle involves the following stages:

1 Flattening after boiling
2 Trimming
3 Shaping with dry heat
 3.1 Bulking up the horn
 3.2 Forming the neck and heel
 3.3 Setting the shape of the grip
 3.4 Forming the out curl on the nose if handle style requires one
4 Filing to final shape (except neck)
5 Joining handle to shaft
6 Filing neck to match shaft
7 Finishing

A BENDING JIG used for forming bufflo horn after boiling.

Horns like ramshorn become pliable only through the careful application of heat. Staghorn, by the way, is more like bone and cannot be shaped in this way at all.

BOILING HORN PRIOR TO FLATTENING.

Boiling in water or even in oil will soften the entire horn but this would mean that all the various shaping stages described below would need to be done in one go. Were you to reheat a previous stage it would revert to its original shape. Boiling is therefore to be recommended only for the first stage.

1 **Flattening** This involves bringing all your material into one plane by removing any curl in the horn. Boiling, or rather first simmering in water, will make the entire horn soft enough to be flattened between two steel or hardwood plates in a large strong vice. Steel plates have the advantage that they will draw

the heat out of the horn more quickly. Cooling can further be speeded up by squirting a mist of water onto the horn from a plastic spray gun. Some stickdressers have constructed a large frame press for pressing their horn using an hydraulic car jack for power.

Once your flattened horn has cooled off a little it can be removed from your equipment. Depending on ambient temperature, this can be anything from 10–40 minutes. Then drop your horn into a bucket of cold water to cool off further.

2 **Trimming** This is the stage at which any unwanted horn is removed. This involves any hollow section with less than $\frac{3}{8}$-in. wall thickness all round, and any sharp ridges should be rounded off. The base of the horn should be cut at an angle of roughly 20° up towards the nose. The heel is also pre-shaped along the back but with a curved and not a straight cut. This trimming greatly eases the work involved in later stages.

Even the solid part of, say, a ramshorn will contain an inner softer core which is much whiter. This is variously known as 'flint' or 'gawk' and it is part of a stickdresser's craft that however the horn is worked, this should never be allowed to show on the surface of the finished handle.

Equally, horn has a discernible grain and on a finished handle this should always follow the same line as the handle shape. That is to say you should never see the line of the grain run at an angle down the neck. It would immediately indicate that the neck has been formed by cutting the shape out of the flattened horn.

3 **Shaping** — with dry heat. Were the entire horn to be heated again, you would undo all previous work. So from now on we heat only the actual part we wish to bend at each stage. Some people use a small meths burner, others a modern electric paint-stripper gun, but most now use bottled gas burners set to a mild red flame. The intense blue flame would cause too much scorch and the resulting case-hardening would make it difficult for further heat to penetrate

into the centre of the horn. Scorch can further be reduced by brushing a light oil onto the section being worked on. The essence of bending horn is a) to be patient when heating to allow the heat slowly to penetrate right into the centre, and b) once you are ready to do the actual shaping not to lose time – this means having all you need ready to hand. Experience will teach you that horn that is soft all the way through makes quite a different dull sound when knocked against a hard surface.

3.1 *Bulking up* — Heat the base end of the horn for some 5in. up the horn until it is fully pliable. Squeeze up the hollow section as much as possible using one of the steel plates against the rear jaw of your vice and the 2-in.-dia. post against the inside of the front jaw. Keep moving the horn and squeezing at different points until the hollow begins to close up. A wooden dowel can be used to prevent the walls of the hollow from folding in on themselves.

3.2 *Necking* — If necessary reheat this section of horn. When properly soft form the neck by squeezing it to shape in the vice between two halves of suitable piping. Some horn may squeeze out between your piping, but this welt can be removed later. Continue to use a wooden plug in any sizeable hollow to prevent any inward creasing. Remove this plug and drill out any rubbish before fully tightening up your vice.

Without removing the neck clamp or reheating, set the angle of heel with a shash cramp. It helps to file out the inside of the heel angle as soon as possible to remove any wrinkles which may have formed.

After full cooling remove from vice and grind or rasp the heel and neck roughly to shape.

3.3 *Setting the Grip* — Reheat your horn, not forgetting a touch more oil against scorch. Work always from heel towards nose, squeezing up bulk where necessary and rasping to shape where there may be too much material. If this means that the horn has started to cool off, then apply more heat before forming the inside grip

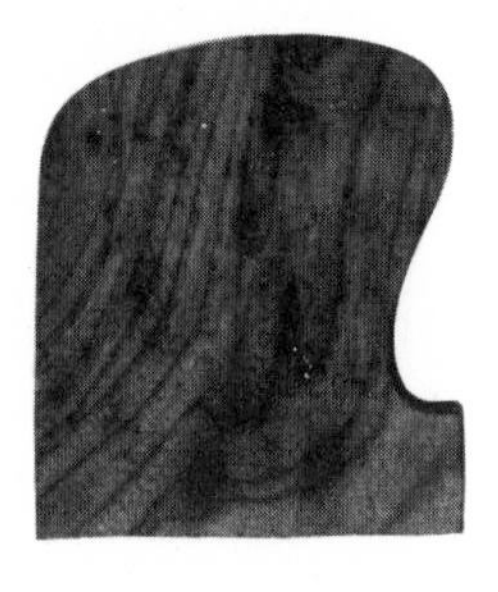

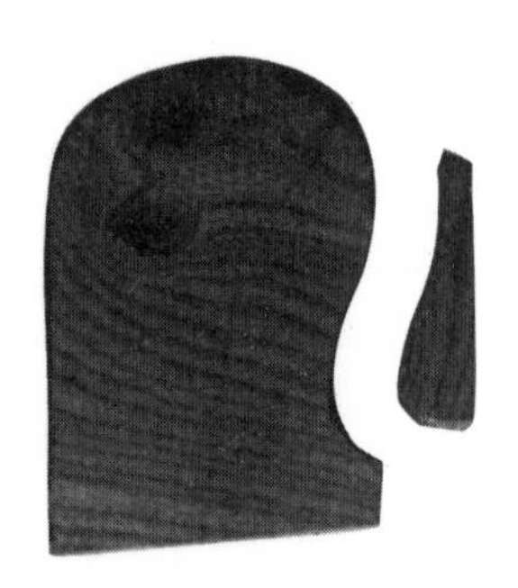

line against a specially shaped wooden former and flatten the whole horn between two plates to prevent any overall twisting. Leave the horn to set between the plates and once removed plunge it into cold water to stop any distortion.

If a curl-in is wanted on the nose this should be set at the same time as the grip line. On the other hand, some market sticks and all proper crooks should have a nose which curls outwards.

3.4 *Out-curl on the Nose*— Once again heat the part of the nose which is to form the curl and set this in the vice between a matching pair of suitably shaped wooden blocks. Once the curl is roughly set, remove the horn from the vice and file out any wrinkles on the inside radius of the curl. The shape can be given a final adjustment by judicious use of the vice jaws or the round-nose pliers.

It is at this stage that a fault will invariably creep in which can totally spoil a stick. That is 'nose droop' caused by heat moving back up the horn and causing the grip line to sag slightly. This must be corrected before the handle is again set between two plates in the vice to flatten it, using wedges to adjust the position of the nose.

Liberal use of water from a spray bottle will help to speed up setting times at all stages.

4 **Filing to Shape** A certain amount of material will have been removed during previous stages but now comes the point at which we have to look at a handle with a more critical eye and with a rasp obtain overall smooth lines and curves. The thickest part of the handle should be at the nose end of the grip with an even taper over the heel back to the joint and also forward down to the nose. Do not take off too much from the neck until the next step is complete.

5 **Shanking** A suitable shaft should now be selected which will complement the handle to give a visually pleasing overall appearance but which will also fall nicely to hand and is not clumsy.

The joint can either be level or at a slope. Neither is very difficult provided certain precautions are taken. Refer to the section 'Jointing' for full details.

6 **Tapering the Neck** From now on you are faced with the slight problem of working on an object not six inches long but four feet or more. I have solved this for myself by making a simple bracket of wood which can be clamped to any table or bench. This 'working rack' allows me to rest the stick horizontally and to work on any part whilst holding it firm with my left hand.

Final rasping to shape should now be done to match the line of the neck to the shaft. There is a danger if care is not taken that you will file into the bark of the shaft. This can be touched up with woodstain felt tip pens, but it is best to try and avoid such blemishes.

Enough material should be left after rasping to allow for further removal during the later finishing stages. These consist of progressively finer files and sandings. The aim of each stage is to remove the scratches and grooves from previous work. After rasping I usually use a medium-cut file, followed by 120-grit sanding pads and then 180-grit. My sanding pads consist of a 2 × 1 batten onto which I first tack some thin foam rubber and over this is fixed the abrasive cloth. The foam sandwich seems to shape itself better to round handles. Another very useful tip is to nail a piece of old carpet to your working rack on which the sanding pad can be wiped clear of dust. A dust-clogged pad does not work well.

An alternative to sanding pads now available from some suppliers is a fibrous abrasive pad made by 3M. It comes in coarse (blue colour), medium (red) and fine (grey). Their main advantage is that they will not clog and that they will shape themselves to the object being worked on.

The 3M grey fibre pad effectively replaces what would normally be the next stage and that is rubbing down with 0 or 00 wire wool. After this I always turn to 0000 wire wool but, at a pinch, a Brillo Pad will do. Even 'Jif' is used by some stickdressers but the strong smell of ammonia rather puts me off.

If you have reached this stage during the evening, leave it until the next morning – take your stick outside and examine your finish. It is very rare for me not to find all sorts of blemishes and scratches that need further work before giving the handle a final finish of wax buffed to a nice shine,

I would plead with you not to cut corners by varnishing your horn. You lose the very fine feel of this material – as a Cumbrian farmer put it 'That's as bad as trying to milk a cow with gloves on.'

JOINTING

The traditional way of joining handle to shank, particularly among stickdressers, is to dowel down the top of the stick to a shoulder and then to glue this into a hole in the handle. Too many sticks fracture at this point for me to find the method at all reliable. I always use a reinforcing pin some 5in. long and at least $\frac{1}{4}$in. diameter. Engineers' studding is available in these dimensions and has a metal screw thread along its entire length. It is normally of mild steel, which has the advantage that one can tweak it slightly to line up the joint surfaces neatly. Naturally high-tensile steel can be used. It can most easily be obtained as fencing bolts from which the hook end must be cropped.

Roughly one-third of the studding goes up into the handle and two-thirds down into the shank. Drill a push-fit hole into the parts to be joined. The glue will key into the thread and make a good bond. To improve this

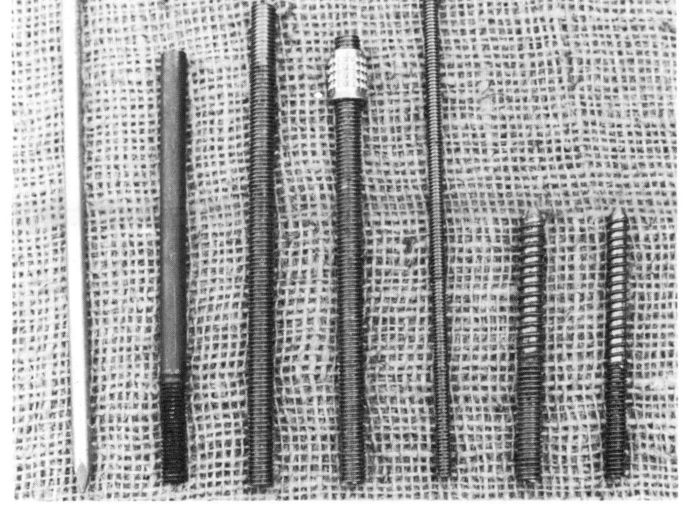

HANDLE PINS
left to right:
1. Six Inch Nail – NOT recommended.
2. Cropped Coach Bolt – minimum $\frac{1}{4}$ ins. diameter.
3. Allthread (Studding) 8 mm recommended.
4. Allthread with Insert for very shallow handles.
5. Allthread – too thin and will bend.
6/7. Dowel Screws – both sizes too short.

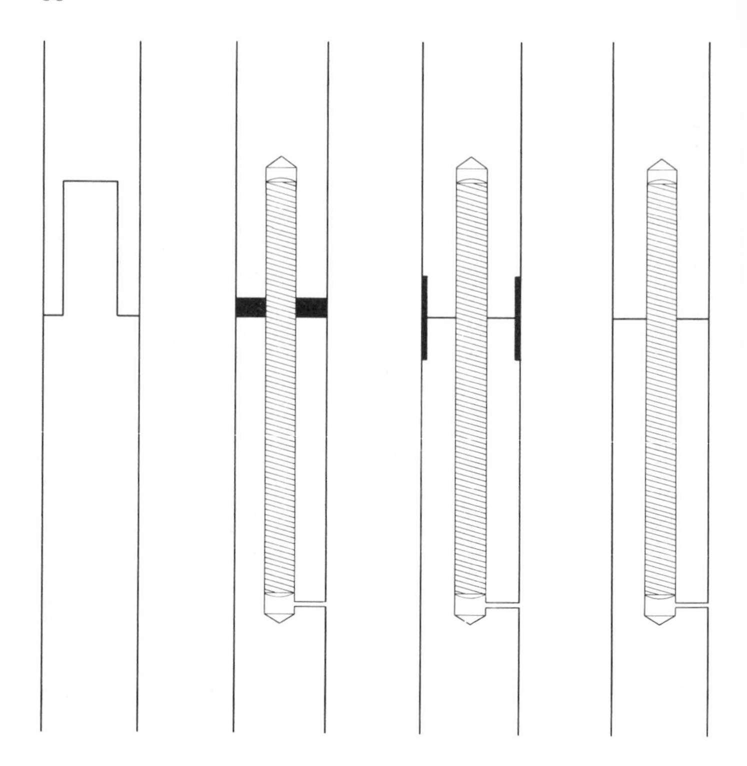

TYPES OF JOINT BETWEEN HANDLE AND SHANK
left to right: 1. Peg Joint – formed from shaft.
2. Spacer J. – a disc of horn & wood.
3. Collar J. – covering the join.
4. Plain J. – best for wood shaft & handle.

bonding, degrease the studding with acetone or lighter fluid. The best type of glue is two-part epoxy, such as Araldite, with no discernible difference, in my experience, between the fast or slow setting types in terms of bond strength. If you have several sticks to glue up at the same time you should definitely use the slow-setting type as the rapid glue will start to set after the second or third stick.

Brass inserts are available, the internal thread of which matches the thread of the studding. These are intended for use only on handles where there is little 'meat' for the joint. They are too short to use for break-down joints on 'travelling sticks'. There are special all-brass joints available for this purpose with longer sections, more resistant to sideways forces and these have proved most useful for long sticks which have to be disassembled on occasion.

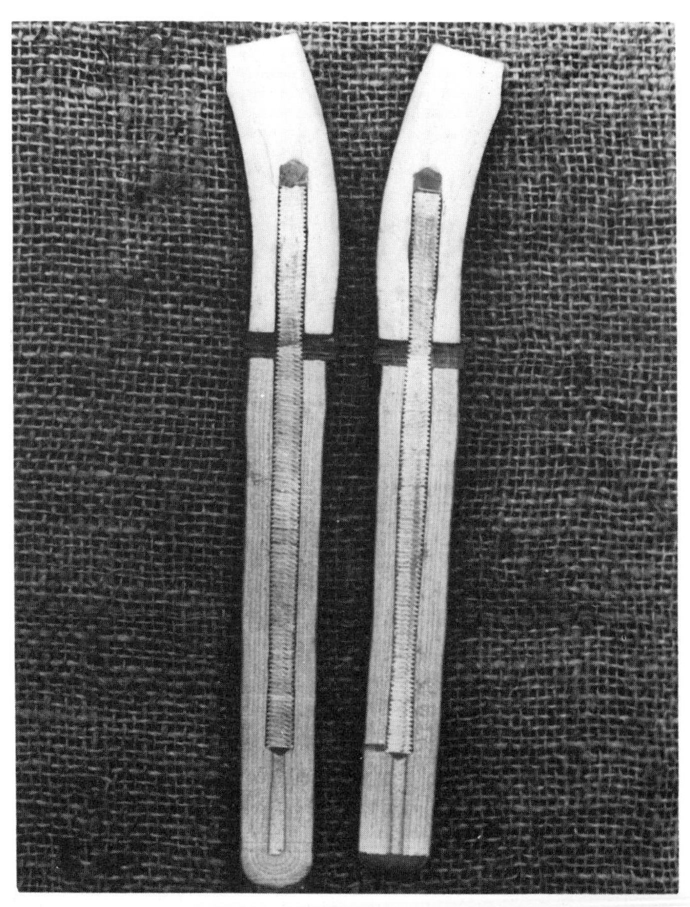

A SPACER JOINT CUT IN HALF.

There is a particular problem when joining staghorn handles. All European staghorn has a hard outer layer but a very soft mushy inner. This I consider too suspect to give a reliable joint and therefore drill out some of the pith with a spade drill and glue in a short length of dowel of the same diameter. Into this I then glue the studding in the normal way to ensure a more secure joint.

To hold the joint in place while the glue is setting, I have seen many and various methods. Necessity being the mother of invention, I have found that a large bulldog clip on the handle and another on the shank with strong rubber bands stretched in between are the most effective. Any sideways pull that may be required can be achieved by wedging a cork or piece of wood under the rubber bands.

DRILLING PIN HOLES.

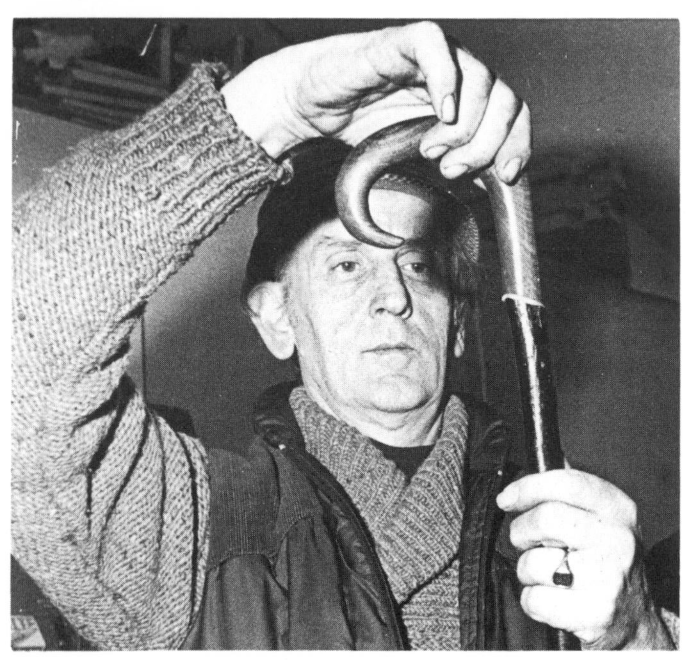

GLUING UP.

STAGHORN (l.-r.) European with soft pith; European plugged with dowel prior to drilling; Indian Sambar with firm centre.

No handle should be finished on the neck until it has been joined to the shank, when it can be tapered down exactly to match the shank. On some handles such as staghorn this is not possible because of the difficulty of 'working' the material. In this case a spacer of buffalo or oxhorn is fitted before gluing up, between the handle and the shank. When filed down after the glue has set, this provides a neat shoulder and helps to set the stick off as something special.

If a collar is to be used on the stick it is obvious that this must be fixed before gluing. Collars are best let into the wood of both the shank and the handle to give a smooth surface over the whole joint. Special brass collars in various sizes are available for this which are very thin walled and will partly flex to shape.

STICK WORKING PACK

FINISHES

Even fully seasoned wood rapidly absorbs moisture from the surrounding atmosphere and must be given some form of protective coating to reduce this. Coating agents can be broadly divided into waxes, oils, lacquers and varnishes.

WAXES

These are not really durable enough on their own for our purpose although they can be used as a sealing coat over other finishes or to revive old sticks. On the other hand,

BUFFING with Caranuba Wax.

for horn, wax finishes are unsurpassed and varnish is not only unnecessary but almost a shame since you lose the feel of the material. Horn takes 14 years to rot underground, and there is no reason at all to varnish it. It is far better to finish with a buffing of carnauba wax. This is a very hard wax obtained from the Brazilian palm tree and normally sold in hard bars. In case of difficulty use a good brand of furniture wax preferably containing a good portion of beeswax. Briwax is one very good brand.

OILS

One usually thinks of linseed oil first. It is vital never, repeat never, to use natural linseed oil in stickmaking because it still contains impurities which prevent it from drying out or oxidising. Always use so-called 'boiled linseed oil'. Actually it never was boiled but only heated to the point at which if one dipped a feather into it, the feather would shrivel up. Today the removal of impurities is achieved chemically.

There is nothing like boiled linseed oil to bring out the grain of wood although it does darken it slightly. Only a few woods are not enhanced by a coating of linseed, such as lime and some other very light woods. It works well on most British woods such as elm, walnut, yew etc.

Boiled linseed oil also has the added advantage that it provides a better key into any wood for varnishes, most of which have it as a component. Do remember, however, that boiled linseed oil still takes several days fully to dry out. If varnish is applied too soon it will take a long time to harden off. Linseed oil alone can only be described at best as 'showerproof' but not waterproof. One must either varnish over it or use one of the waterproof oils combined with linseed. This combination is available in brands of gunstock oils such as Birchwood Casey which contain Tung Oil.

LACQUERS

These can generally be dismissed as quite unsuitable for stickmaking. They are intended only for indoor applications.

VARNISHES

These cannot be bettered for finishing the wood on sticks. Most outdoor varnishes are good, since they not only contain a UV inhibitor which slows down chemical ageing from daylight, but also extra plasticisers to allow the varnish to flex with the wood. The best are the so-called spar or yacht varnishes which are made to cope with the most severe conditions. Unfortunately spar varnishes are usually available only in gloss or super-gloss. The gloss can, however, always be cut back to a satin-like surface with '0000' wire wool once the varnish has fully set.

STICK LENGTHS

The best length for a walking stick is measured from the floor to the corner of the hip joint – that is where the actual joint projects, not the top of the hip bone. Appropriate shoes should be worn when measuring as this can influence length, particularly for ladies. In measuring for a stick the important factor is actually the angle of the elbow. If this is too straight the stick will not give the required lift. If the elbow is too bent the stick will be tiring to use. Comfort is the key factor. If in doubt, take off less – you can always take off more but never put it back.

Longer sticks such as thumbsticks, market sticks and shepherds' crooks should be measured so that when held naturally the forearm is at least horizontal. This is a minimum angle and can be increased upwards by preference or if the terrain will be rough or hilly.

Other factors apply to specialist sticks. Woodland stalking poles for example should be at least as tall as the person using them. Wading sticks should come to the shoulder, and dipping hooks may need to be some eight to ten feet long.

Most stickmakers will be faced at one time or other by someone who has inherited granny's old stick. Now grannies for some reason tend not to be very tall and the stick will almost always be too short and the stickmaker will be asked if he can make it longer again'. Never give any guarantees if you are asked because the whole exercise is a compromise between strength and balance. Some form of pin will be required to reinforce the joint but if this is too heavy, the stick will seem like a pendulum.

FERRULES

Let us first clearly define what we mean by a ferrule when talking of walking sticks. The term applies exclusively to the fitting at the bottom of a stick which prevents rapid wear and provides a good hold on the ground.

Ferrules can be made of brass, steel, ivory, rubber or some form of horn. Very occasionally they are found in silver and even then, usually with a steel tip. The most common form in use in Britain consists of a brass cup, usually with a dull lacquer finish and a steel plate at the base for extra wear. They are normally available in sizes from half-inch to the full inch in one-eighth-inch steps. Interim sizes can also be obtained. Someone, a long while back, had the brilliant idea of trying to simplify ferrule sizes by creating nominal sizes based on sixteenths of an inch. Thus $\frac{9}{16}$ in. became size 9, and $\frac{3}{4}$ in. became size 12. These nominal sizes are still in conventional use today but it does get confusing when one arrives at the inevitable in-between sizes of say $8\frac{3}{4}$ (which equals $\frac{35}{64}$ in.). These minute in-between sizes are really quite unnecessary since one can always cut a slight shoulder into the stick to fit the next lowest size.

The table below gives nominal sizes as used in Britain for ferrules, caps and collars, with imperial and metric equivalents:

	in.	*mm*	
Nominal	*Imperial*	*Metric*	
6	$\frac{3}{8}$	9.5	Used mostly on
7	$\frac{7}{16}$	11+	umbrellas
8	$\frac{1}{2}$	12.5	
9	$\frac{9}{16}$	14.5	
10	$\frac{5}{8}$	16-	
11	$\frac{11}{16}$	17.5	
12	$\frac{3}{4}$	19+	
13	$\frac{13}{16}$	20.5+	
14	$\frac{7}{8}$	22+	
15	$\frac{15}{16}$	24+	
16	1 in.	25.5-	

To size and ferrule a stick, measure it against the person it is intended for by holding it against them upside down. Mark the length, allowing for any handle projections as

FERRULES
left to right:
1. Plate F. – as used on shooting sticks.
2. Continental Spike F. – chrome on steel.
3. European Screw-in Spike F. – steel.
4. Staghorn (Sambar) F.
5. Oxhorn F.
6. British Brass Ferrule.
7. Piping – adequate but not very neat.

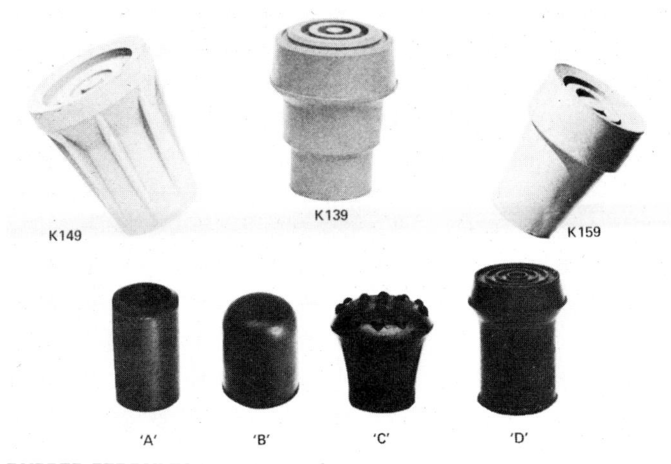

RUBBER FERRULES in various styles.

on thumbsticks, trim to length and taper the bottom with a knife or rasp. The taper must be shaped to fit the taper of the inside of the ferrule. If you do not have a ferrule of quite the right size, use a slightly smaller one and cut a shoulder into the wood. Then tap the ferrule onto the stick. You will feel when the stick bottoms in the cup, which is important or it will later work loose again. With a nail or punch then make three dimples round the ferrule about one-eighth of an inch below the rim. Three, because this prevents the ferrule from pivoting loose as would be the case with only two. Dimpling is better than pinning because there is less chance of splitting the wood. Some people prefer to use epoxy resin for fixing their ferrules, which is alright until you come to renew them!

Trim away any fibres or bark raised by the rim in tapping on, and the job is done.

During research for this book some months ago I came across a series of photographs of a stick factory, sadly now no longer in existence. Among these was a tool we now associate only with clog makers, which is known by them as a clogging iron and more generally as a stock knife or shave hook. It took some time to work out what it was being used for by a stickmaker. I eventually worked out, with the help of some bright friends, that it was a tool for fitting ferrules. The illustration shows the shave hook I had made by a blacksmith and which, after some considerable amending, works remarkably well and fast. There must still be some genuine old ones about but they may not be recognised for what they are. Shave hooks are in fact a highly effective way of removing wood very fast on account of the immense leverage achieved. In their day they were used in all sorts of trades.

FERRULE FITTING TOOL reconstructed by the author from a photograph he discovered in an old collection.

The photograph shows the blade in use for tapering down the end of the stick. Between the blade and the hook was a short pin which was used for crimping on the ferrule.

A final thought on fitting ferrules. We go to all sorts of trouble to varnish and finish a stick and then when it comes to fitting the ferrule, we cut back into bare wood at the very end which will get wet first. A spot of varnish at this stage will certainly do no harm and even help to lock the ferrule in place. This could even be out of your wife's old clear nail varnish bottle kept handy for this purpose.

SELLING YOUR STICKS

There are many ways of passing on your finished product once you have run out of friends to give them to. Some people even progress to selling to their friends and colleagues at work. The basic decision you must make is whether you sell direct to the public or via the retail trade. The first will give you possibly higher returns for considerable effort and the latter, lower returns but not quite such hard work.

If you opt for the latter, your first step must be to find some shops in your area interested in selling crafts of a local origin. Tourist spots and National Trust properties with a gift shop are also useful outlets. Visit them regularly during the season and offer to top up their stock. Be clear about the terms on which you are prepared to supply your sticks. Sale-or-return does you very little good and even Monthly Account can cause you major headaches. The only realistic terms are Payment On Delivery. The customer gets the equivalent of cash settlement discount by having a free delivery. Each retail outlet will have particular preferences and certain items which sell particularly well, sometimes without any logical reason. Allow for these in the range of sticks you make. After all it doesn't do to produce only sticks which you like but which will not sell.

The alternative way to find a home for your products is to sell direct to the public at craft shows and other such events. Whilst each show can make for a really hard day's work, the returns can be greater and it can also be great fun if you enjoy meeting people. Small local village fairs can be alright but tend to be rather more of a public relations exercise. It often pays to join a local craft group, if there is one in your area.

There are really three benefits in attending craft shows. The first, naturally, is to sell since at the end of the day making a profit is rather important. Secondly, they will get you better known and quite a lot of orders will come as a follow-on from people who have picked up your card or leaflet. The third factor I always call my 'perks' and that is to meet a great many very interesting people, including other stickmakers.

Fair organisers vary greatly in their approach to such events. You have to trust them initially to spend a significant part of your stand fee on promoting the event. If they don't bring enough paying customers through the gates to make it worth while, everyone is going to lose out. Except, that is, for the organiser who can usually find enough hungry craftsmen the following year to carry on. At the beginning you will have no choice but to trust to luck and book a few events. Obviously, you keep well away in future from any you have found unsatisfactory. It would be unrealistic to suggest that all organisers are bad news; quite the opposite, but there are some doubtful ones about.

A Craft Fair in London.

Other craftsmen at these shows are almost all only too willing to help and advise. The atmosphere at craft fairs is nearly always a good one in that every craftsman respects others for their ability. This is not so much the case at other types of show.

Finally, remember that even though our materials are cheap and easily obtained, do not underestimate the value of your end-product. As you progress and improve do ask a fair price for your sticks. This should include a realistic factor for the total time you have spent on the stick. And that should include the time you spent finding it in the first place. Good Luck!

GLOSSARY

A GLOSSARY OF TERMS

Ambulist – reputed to be the name for a collector of sticks whilst it actually only refers to walking (the Latin '*ambulare*'). There is no related Latin word meaning a walking stick, and ambulist ought to mean 'one who is in the habit of walking' as somnambulist equals sleep-walker. An alternative word would be BACTROPHOLIST which is more accurate than the third possibility, RHABDOPHOLIST, which means a collector of staffs of office. The collecting of walking sticks would therefore be BACTROPHILY

Antipugilism – the art of fighting with sticks

Balance – in a stick refers to how well it carries. The shank should be straight and must balance the head/handle. It should also have an easy taper from top to bottom. The whole stick must feel lively and not 'dead' in the hand

Cane – the generic name in the US for a walking stick as it was in Britain about the time of Henry VIII. Now relates in Britain only to sticks made from imported exotic woods or turned sticks

Carrying Stick – shaped rather like a shallow 'W' for carrying objects over the shoulder, the weight being on the back, counterbalanced by one hand in front

Chinning the Cosh (or 'Kosts') – a term used by travelling people meaning to 'cut a stick'

Collars and **Bands** – used to tidy up or decorate the joint between handle and shank (*see also* **Spacer**)

Congo Pearl – nothing to do with Africa, but a method of causing interesting, small, regularly spaced knobs on a stick. This is done by wounding it with a special instrument during growth, the knobs being the resulting scars. Mostly used on chestnut

Coppice – a very ancient way of harvesting wood by cutting back to ground level every 8-12 years. Most hardwoods coppice well, whilst most conifers will not. This crop cycle can carry on almost indefinitely, having been practised in certain woods in this country for hundreds of years. Pollarding differs only in that the tree, usually willow, is cut back to the main stem about six feet above ground level to prevent cattle and deer from browsing on the new shoots

Cleek – means crook but refers only to the leg crook, which is used for catching sheep by the hind leg

Cricket – is reputed to originate from a game played by shepherds' boys with their crooks; the wicket being a sheep's wicket and originally consisting of 2 stumps

Cromach – the Gaelic name for a crook (ref. the song 'Road to the Isles')

Crook – a handle bent into a full semi-circle. *See also* **Shepherds' Crooks**

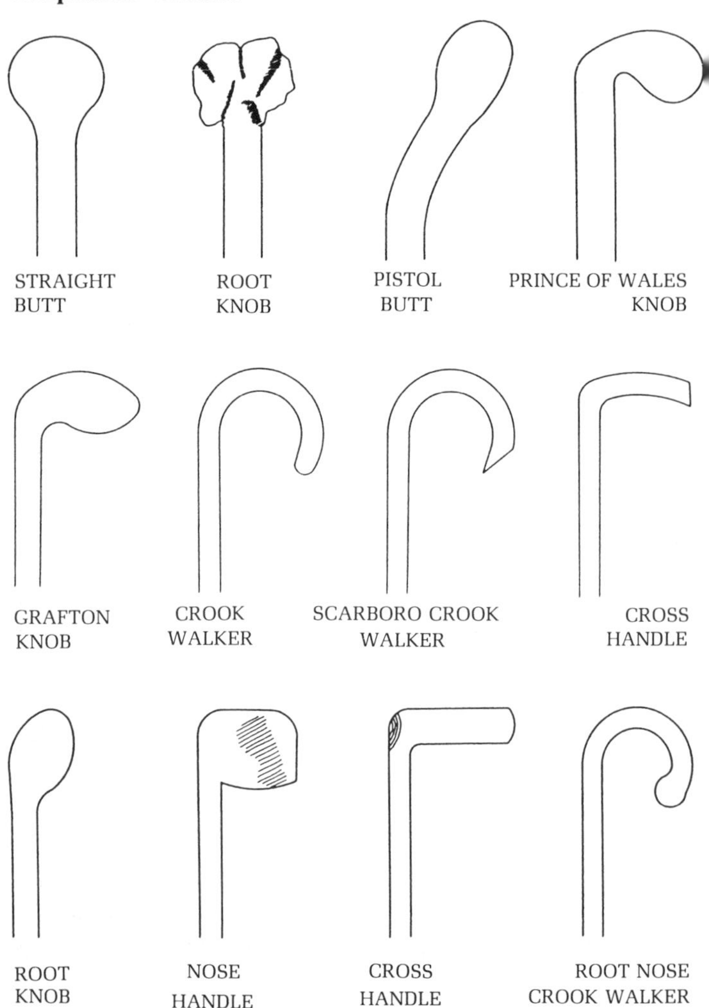

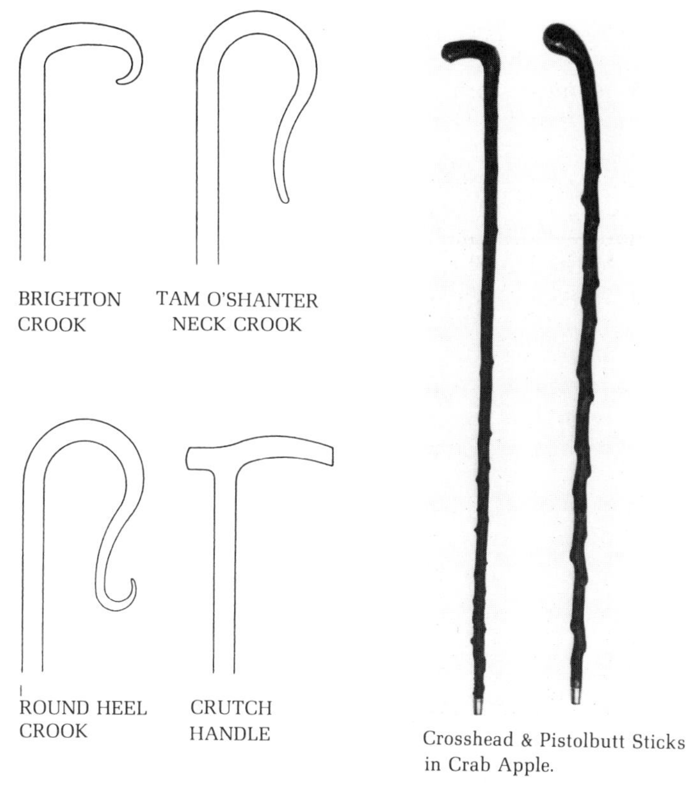

Crosshead & Pistolbutt Sticks in Crab Apple.

Various Natural Handles.

Cross-head – refers to stick handles shaped like an upside-down 'L' in wood
Crown – the very highest part of a stick at the top of the handle
Crozier – another Scottish name for a crook
Deputy Stick, Miner's – used for measuring work done, roof heights and safety, is always exactly 36 in. long. Made by tradition from ash with virtually no taper down the shank, a parallel-sided thicker handle and with a special ferrule to take a gas-testing lamp. On the continent miners carry, as symbol of their occupation, a stick with a stylised axe-head handle
Dipping Hook — a neck crook designed first to push the sheep's head under, and then to lift it clear of, the dipping bath
Distaff – a cleft stick holding wool or flax for spinning by hand, consequently 'women's work'
Distresser

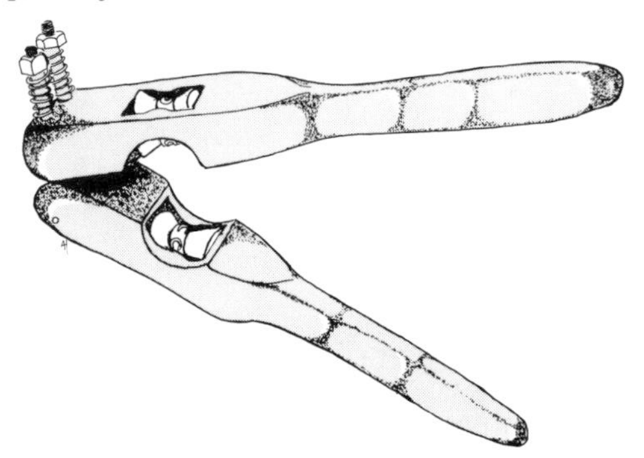

This old instrument, known as a "distresser" was used to scar the bark of Sweet Chestnut whilst it was still growing. The resulting knobly stick becomes a "Pearl Congo" stick.

Fancy — a shepherd's crook with carved decoration. Quite often this is a thistle on the nose
Ferrule — refers only to the fitting at the bottom of the stick to reduce wear and prevent slipping. Can be made of many materials but in Britain usually of a brass cup with a steel tip
Finneal – in the US means ferrule
Fire the Hand — an undesirable stick will 'fire the hand' by having too rough a handle
Fittings – metal parts used in stickmaking, including ferrules, collars, badges, nose mounts, slipper mounts and metal tubes for lining thong holes

Fit up – trade term for a shank varnished and fitted with ferrule before the handle is mounted
Flaming – lightly scorching a stick to give it colour
Flint — the central white core in ramshorn extending into the solid part. Also known as 'Gawk'
Float – a special single-cut file for working wood and horn. Horn workers use a float with a curved edge known as a Graille
Fuming – the staining of a stick by using ammonia fumes
Gape – *see* **Mouth**
Gibbey Sticks – made by the fictitious Mr Jogglebury Crowdey in *Mr Sponge's Sporting Tour* by R.S. Surtees; consisted of carved caricatures of famous people
Gipsy Sticks – are gorse (or furze) sticks traditionally sold by them on Epsom Down on Derby Day
Graille – *see* **Float**
Heel – the point where the handle turns from horizontal to vertical towards the shank. Can be angular or a regular curve. Sometimes is understood to include the vertical section down to the joint
Horse – is a heavy board propped at an angle of about 60 degrees with notches down each side. These are used for levering sticks straight after steaming. *See also* **Shave Horse**
Knob Kerrie – from the Afrikans 'Knopkierie', a short stick with a knobbed head, used as a weapon
Lambing Hook — a term used in the Borders for 'Neck Crook'
Leg Cleek – usually made of metal by local blacksmiths in a wide variety of shapes. Can also be made of horn or wood. The width of the mouth should be equal to the diameter of an old halfpenny (25mm) for lambs, or an old penny (31mm) for adult sheep
Line – is the curve of the handle as seen in silhouette
Linstock – used by gun captains to fire cannon. They were poles with a slow match at the end
Mouth – or Gape, is the distance between the shank and the inside of the nose at its narrowest point
Nose – the end part of the handle or crook furthest away from the shank
Nose Mounts – are rounded metal caps fitted to the end of a handle. Some have a tail extending up the handle and

are known as Long Nose Mounts

Pad – an alternative name for a ferrule used mainly in Scotland

Pearl Congo – *see* **Congo Pearl**

Pull-Down – a particular type of stick, usually of sweet chestnut, on which the handle is steamed and bent over at an angle of 90 degrees. Originally may have been formed by hanging from a barn beam with a weight 'pulling down'

Pyecombe – a small village near Brighton long famous for a particular shape of iron leg cleek

Reducing — a trade term for tapered wood shafts. These are generally not turned between centres on a lathe but reduced with special rounder planes (*see* 'To Bark or Not')

Rods, Poles and **Perches** – a traditional unit of measurement often relating to hedges and boundaries. Equals 5½yd or 5m

Rhabdopholist – an alternative and perhaps better name for a stick collector than ambulist. But this term refers more to collecting staffs of office

Scorching *see* **Flaming**

Scrumping Sticks – usually well over three feet long with the handle forming a hook. Boys of all ages for the use of . . . Also useful for collecting blackberries

Shank – or shaft of a stick — is the section from the handle to the ground, usually of wood

Shave Horse – a clamping bench used to hold lengths of wood or sticks while shaving them down with a draw knife or Surform shaver

Squoyle — a poaching stick with a lead weight in the handle

Shepherds' Crooks – also known as the shepherds' long arm, are used to catch and isolate individual sheep. They can take the following forms:

Neck Crooks are only just four fingers wide at the mouth. In the northern counties of England and in Scotland they are mostly made of ramshorn but more frequently now from water buffalo horn due to the shortage of more traditional materials. In Wales the neck crook is commonly made of hazel shank and its attached root or stem block. A cheap form of neck crook is also

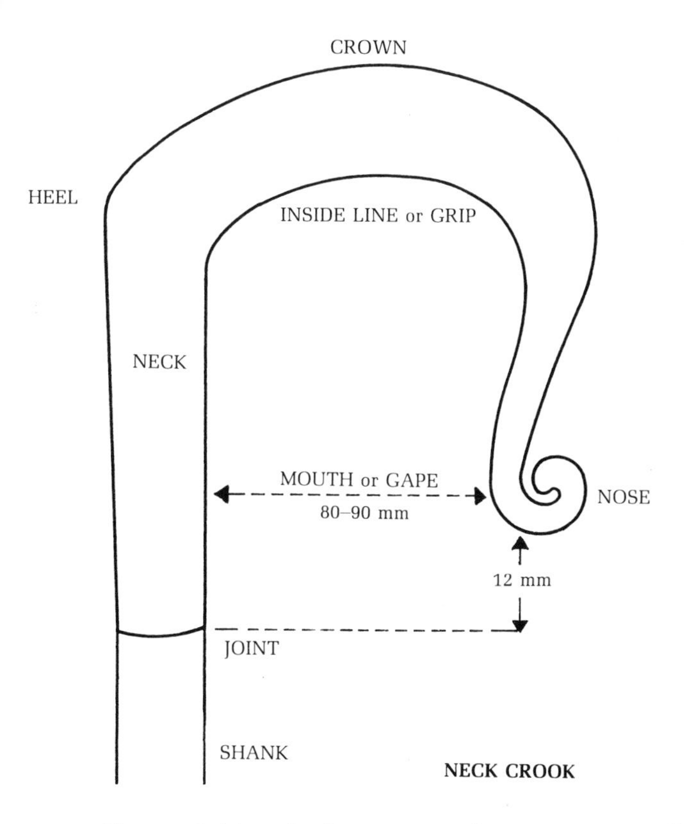

NECK CROOK

generally available which is steam bent commercially from various woods. God forbid, there are also on the market now crooks made entirely out of aluminium tubing

Leg Cleeks were used mostly in the southern counties of England and were almost always made by local blacksmiths in very great variety of styles and shapes. Old ones are still occasionally found in hedgerows. Old gun barrels were sometimes used but so were hazel root blocks and horn

Market Sticks derive from shepherds' crooks but are much more elaborate and used only as a social symbol. Known as Scottish hooks in some areas

Dipping Hooks enable shepherds to push down on the sheep's neck with one side of the hook and then to lift the head clear of the dipping fluid with the other. Usually made of iron but sometimes of wood

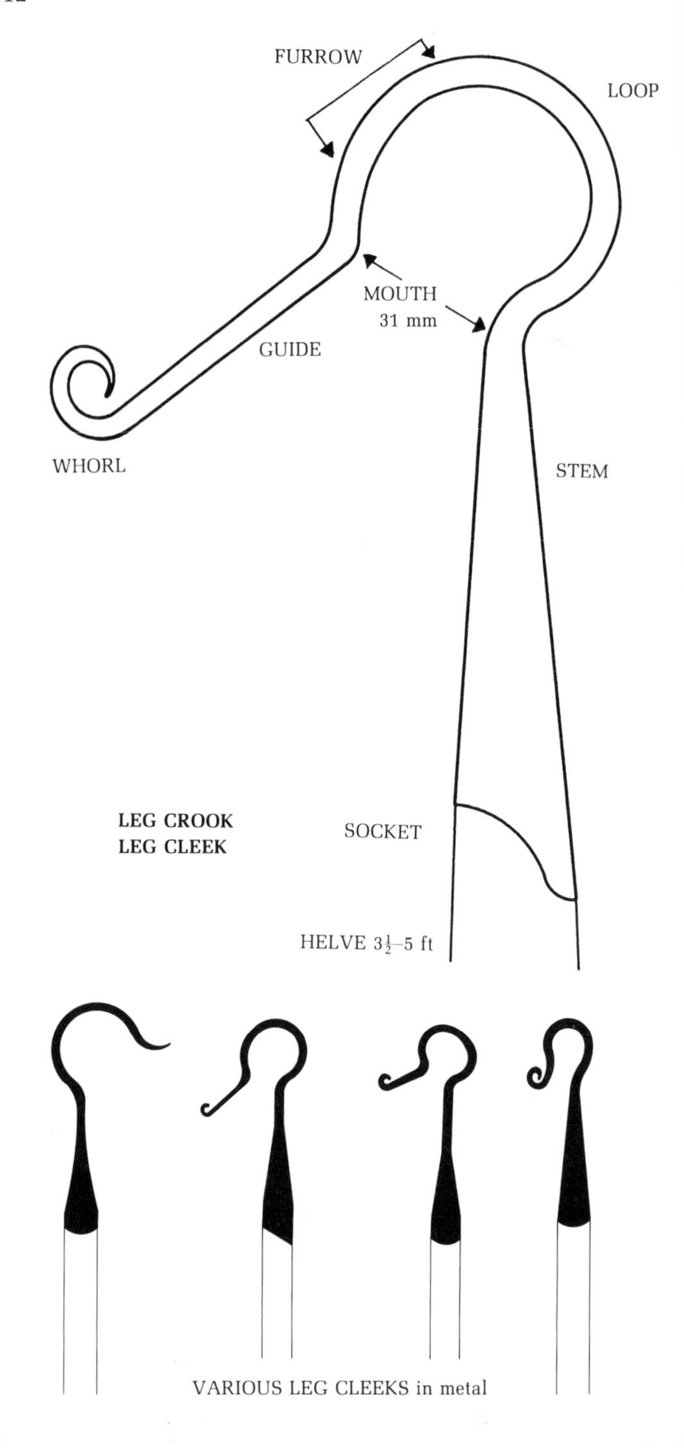

VARIOUS LEG CLEEKS in metal

COMBINED LEG & NECK CROOK
in metal from the Romney Marshes.

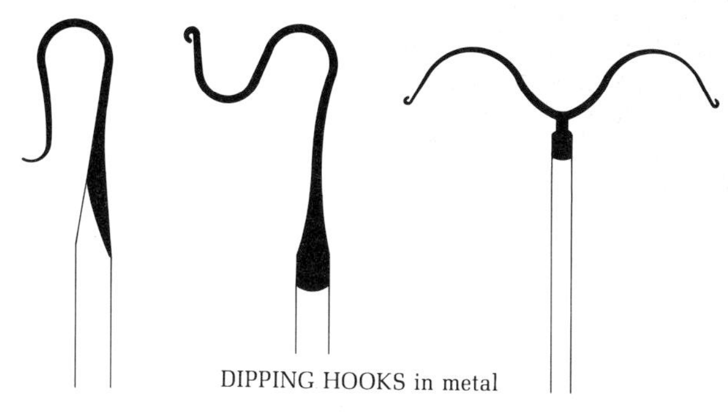

DIPPING HOOKS in metal

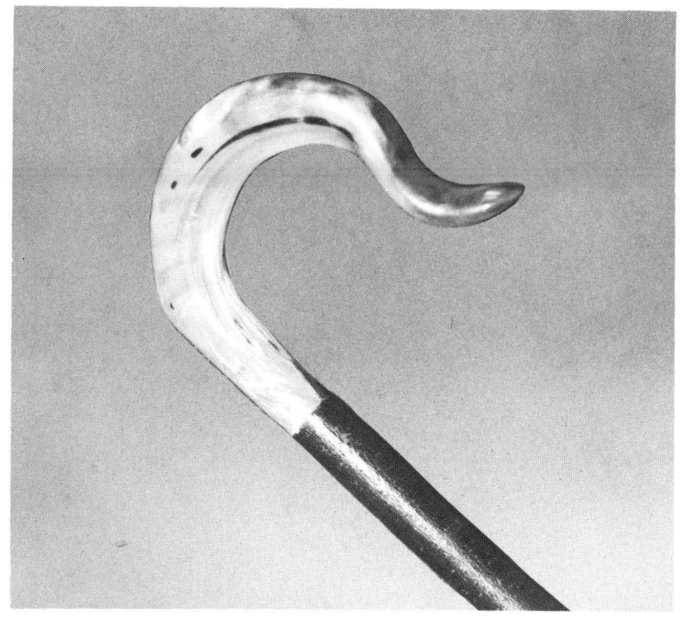

MARKET STICK.

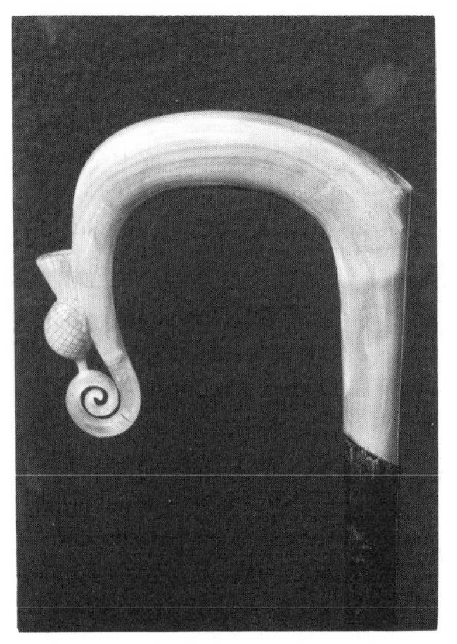

A fine example of a "fancy crook" with a thistle carved on the nose.

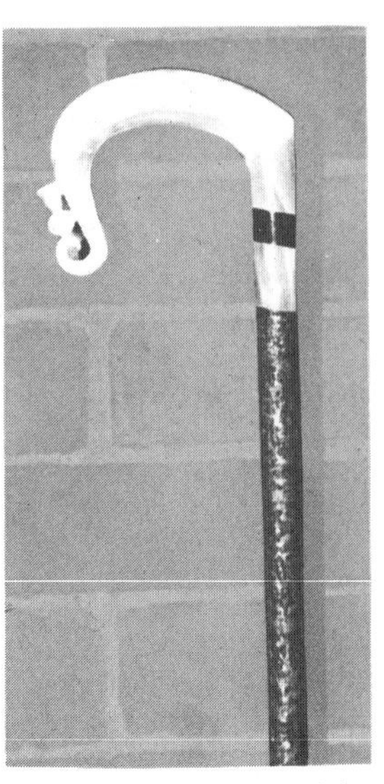

A dressed Crook by Mr. A. Brooks of Colne.

SHEPHERDS' CROOKS

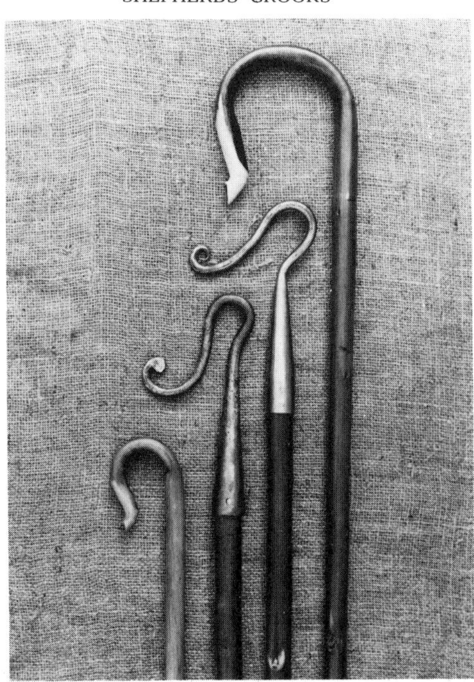

left to right: Chicken Crook – steam bent. Two forged Leg Cleeks. Cheap Neck Crook – steam bent.

Shepherds' Slings – are no longer in use but consisted of a pole at least 3 feet long of ash or hazel, split at the end to make a gap large enough to take a stone. Antler or horn cups were also used to hold the stone. The use of the sling required considerable practice, but once mastered could be used over considerable distances and with great accuracy to protect sheep from attack. No doubt they added to the pot with it if the chance arose
Shillelagh – generally believed to be a hammer-shaped club made of blackthorn. In fact it was originally an oak throwing-stick used to deadly effect on game and other items for the pot. The name itself derives from a village in Co. Wicklow, Eire
Shooting Stick – a walking stick with handles which form a complete loop and which unfold to form a seat. This is used to prop up the backside mostly during country pursuits. Can also incorporate an umbrella

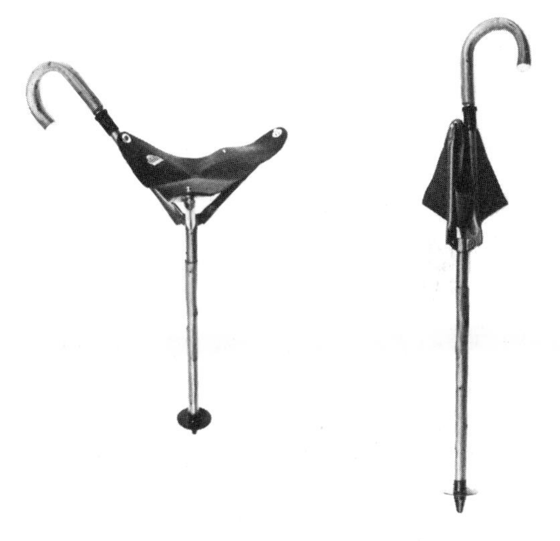

SHOOTING STICK, a very elegant and practical German Seat Stick which is comfortable to sit on and strong when locked closed.

Shotgun Stick – a walking stick incorporating the mechanism of a shotgun. Usually this is the No.3 garden gun (9mm) or .410 gauge. These sticks are not illegal in Britain provided they are handled as a shotgun by someone holding the necessary permits. Their use on the public highway is of course highly illegal since that would constitute the carrying of a concealed weapon

Slipper Mounts – similar to Nose Mounts – are used to cap the end of a handle. Their shape is obliquely flattened at the end

Snake Stick — *see* **Twisty Sticks**

Spacer or **Washer** – used to build the joint between handle and shank. Unlike a collar, it forms a layer between the two with only the fixing pin passing through it.

Spade Sticks – continental shepherds rarely use a crook. Instead they fit a small spade to the end of their staffs with which they flick stones or bits of turf to turn their sheep. They don't even have any herding dogs such as our collies. The alsatian for example is purely a guard dog. *See also* **Thistle Spudder** and **Shepherds' Slings**

Staff – used by running footmen in the late 18th and 19th centuries. Other staffs became symbols of office, for example Black Rod

Stalking Poles – used for stalking deer in woodlands. Hill stalking requires only a normal thumbstick. A stalking pole should be at least as tall as the person using it, have no bright or shiny fittings and terminate in a rubber ferrule. It helps if it can be unscrewed into two sections for transport in vehicles

SUIGI – flame scorched sticks.

Standard, British – There is one British Standard relating to walking sticks. This covers only walking sticks made from sweet chestnut as supplied to the National Health Authorities, under BS 5181:1975
Stickler – originates from Cornish wrestling. Sticklers are the referees, each of whom carries a stick with which to tap when points are scored. The origin of 'A stickler for detail'
Suigi – a method of scorching wood with a clean flame (no soot) to bring out the grain
Sword Sticks – have a concealed blade fitted inside them. It is illegal to carry one in a public place
Symbolism—Most everyday objects have a symbolic significance and the same applies to the walking stick in all its forms and derivations.

The CROOK is the pastoral symbol of the Christian Church. The hook indicates divine power and communication. The spiral shape denotes creative power.
MACES symbolise crushing power or utter destruction and therefore are used as a symbol of ultimate authority.
Even the OAR being derived from the same shape, denotes the idea of creation.
The SCEPTRE is symbolic of the thunderbolt and the phallus. It denotes fertility. Often they terminate in a fleur-de-lis which stands for light and purification.
STAFFS by their straight shape indicate direction and intensity, and also power.
STICKS represent support but also punishment. On the other hand, a BURNT STICK represents death and wisdom.

Other evolutions of the stick are:
The Magician's Wand
The Marshal's Baton
The Swagger Stick
The Conductor's Baton
& many more, all of which are used to indicate some form of authority.

Thistle Spudder – a stick with a small blade fitted at the ferrule end for cutting out thistles and docks at the root. Sometimes also made with a pull-action hook blade on one side edge

Thumbstick – any stick taller than four feet, usually with some form of ledge onto which the thumb can be hooked. Sticks of four feet or more in length are much more common in the British Isles than elsewhere

Tipple Stick – contains a narrow bottle to hold liquid refreshment of the owner's choice. Some even include one or two small drinking cups

Twisty Sticks – these have been distorted in their growth by a spiral constriction caused by honeysuckle.

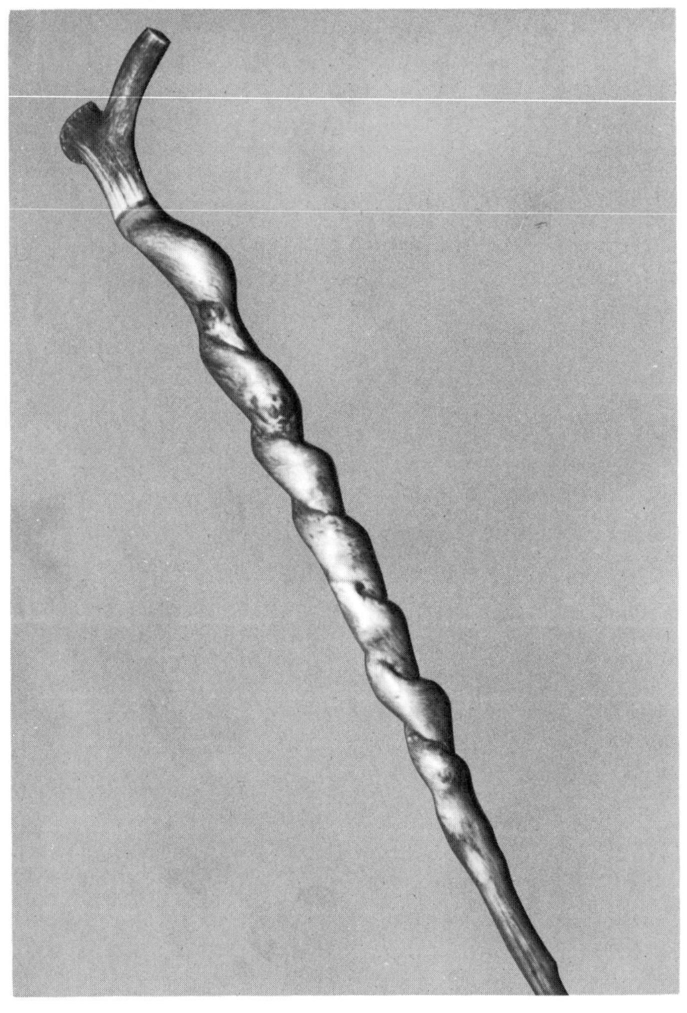

Good example of a "Twisty" Stick. The distortion being caused by Honeysuckle constricting the sapling in growth.

TWISTY STICKS in Ash, Hazel, Peeled Rowan and Raw Cherry.

Much sought after by stickmakers. By the way, the famous Sir Harry Lauder's sticks were not twisty sticks but made from contorted hazel

Wading Staff – should be some five feet high, weighted at the bottom, with a ferrule which will not slip on rock (horn is best) and be fitted with a lanyard to go over the shoulder. Used by fishermen on fast-flowing rivers

Washer – *see* **Spacer**

Washer Sticks – are made entirely from washers of various materials threaded onto a central spine

BIBLIOGRAPHY

There are not many books published about stickmaking, but the following is a list of those that cover the subject, plus some others that provide reference on particular aspects:

SHEPHERDS CROOKS & WALKING STICKS, David Grant & Edward Hart. Dalesman Publishing Co., 1972, 48 pages, illustrated

THE ART OF STICKDRESSING, Norman Tulip. Frank Graham Publ., Newcastle-upon-Tyne 1978, 56 pages, colour plates

FASCINATING WALKING STICKS, A. E. Boothroyd. White Lion Publ., 1973, but now out of print, 204 pages, illustrated

CANE CURIOSA, Catherine Dike. Published privately Geneva 1982, 375 pages, 1650 illustrations

CANES & WALKING STICKS, Kurt Stein. Liberty Cap Books, York, Conn., USA 1974, but now out of print, 175 pages, illustrated

A COMPLETE BOOK OF COUNTRY CRAFTS, Jack Hill. David & Charles, 1979, 254 pages, illustrated

BLACKTHORN, J. M. Douglas. Alloway Publishing, 1984, 80 pages, illustrated

SPAZIERSTOECKE, U. Klever. Callwey, Munich, 1984, 244 pages, illustrated, in German

WALKING STICKS, Edward Hart. Crowood Press, Marlborough, 1986, 96 pages, illustrated

DISCOVERING HORN Paula Hardwick. Lutterworth Press, 1981, 192 pages, illustrated

FIELD GUIDE TO THE TREES AND SHRUBS OF GREAT BRITAIN. Readers Digest, 1981, 304 pages, well illustrated

TECHNIQUES OF CREATIVE WOODCARVING Ian Norbury. Stobart & Son, 1983, 160 pages, illustrated

THE TECHNIQUES OF WOOD SCULPTURE David Orchard. Batsford, 1984, 144 pages with colour

USEFUL ADDRESSES

Magazines

Woodworker, monthly UK, Infonet Ltd, 10-13 Times House, 179 Marlowes, Hemel Hempstead, Herts, HP1 1BB.

Practical Woodworking, monthly UK, King's Reach Tower, Stamford Street, London SE1 9LS.

Woodworking Crafts, quarterly UK, 170 High Street, Lewes, E. Sussex BN7 1YE.

Fine Woodworking, bi-monthly USA, The Taunton Press Inc, Newton, USA CT06470.

We have noted down one or two addresses and other information we thought you might find useful. Inevitably these do change with time, so check before sending any money.

British Stickmakers Guild — Formed in 1984, this guild was open to anyone interested in stickmaking and reached a 1000 members. Recent events within the committee have caused several of us to resign even our membership. It is with great regret that we can no longer recommend it.

International Stick Society — Formed in 1988, this new society aims to bring together collectors of sticks from all over the world. Members receive a yearbook and occasional newsletters. Write to Theo Fossel, 119 Station Road, Beaconsfield, Bucks HP9 1LG, England, for further details.

Walking-Stick News — A periodical newsletter is published for collectors. No charge but a contribution towards postage would only be right. Contact Mr Cecil Curtis, 4051 East Olive Road, Box 231, Pensacola, Florida 32514, USA.

The Cane Collector's Chronicle — Just this morning we have received the first edition of a new newsletter about walking stick collecting. It will cost $30 ($35 from outside USA) and is available from Mrs Linda Beeman, 15 Second Street NE, Washington DC 20002, USA.

Craftsmans Directory for Shows in Britain — Anyone wanting a director of almost all major craft shows would do well to get one from: S.&J. Lance Publications, Brook House, Mint Street, Godalming, Surrey GU7 1HE. (04868 22184).

Silver, Gold & Platinum — These may only be sold in Britain (with very few specific exceptions) if they have been hallmarked. The best guide is 'Bradbury's Book of Hallmarks' available at most bookshops for very little money.

Information on USA Craft Shows (Art Festivals) — A most useful list is published annually; which also grades the shows by region and gives comments: Send $35 to Lawrence Harris, PO Box 142-L, La Veta, Colorado 81055. USA.

International Hallmarks — Are covered in 'Tardy International Hallmarks on Silver'. This book and other items are available by post from: Quicktest, PO Box 180, Watford, WD1 5JD, England.

Mail Order Specialists for Woodworking Books — Stobart & Son Ltd are publishers but also run a very efficient and friendly mail order service. Send for their list: 67-73 Worship Street, London EC2A 2EL, England. (071 247 0501).

Hard-to-Get Tools by Post — A very friendly firm with a vast range of items is: J. Simble & Sons, Queens Road, Watford, Herts WD1 2LD. (Send £1 for their catalogue).

Northern England Stockist — A great many of our specialist items are stocked by Craft Supplies Ltd, Millers Dale, Buxton, Derbys SK11 8SN.

Stickmaking Components now available in North America — Most stickmaking components are now stocked by Theo Fossel Associates, P.O. Box 6894, Alexandria VA 22306-0894, USA.

INDEX

NOTES

NOTES

NOTES